DAD JOKES

DAD JOKES

THE BAD, THE FUNNY, THE PUNNY

JULIAN
FLANDERS

This edition published in 2025 by Arcturus Publishing Limited
26/27 Bickels Yard, 151–153 Bermondsey Street,
London SE1 3HA

AD012162NT

Printed in the UK

CONTENTS

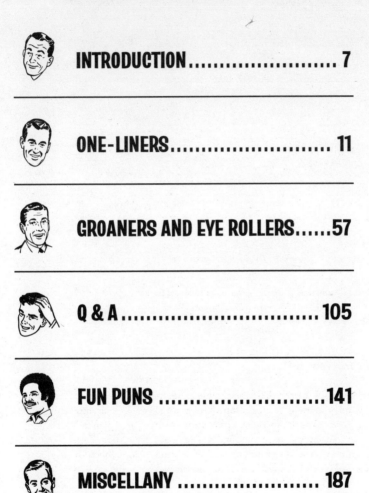

INTRODUCTION

Something funny happens when you become a dad—and it's not just the joy of holding your precious newborn baby and the excitement of starting a new family. One day you're a young man about town, nicely dressed, good haircut, working, socializing, buying the latest tunes, and clubbing on a Friday night. Then the baby bomb goes off, you get lost in nappies, night feeds, prams, not enough sleep, and too much shopping for baby clothes. The next few years rush past, you have no time for anything, least of all laughing, joking, and socializing.

In time—a few years' time—you start to get out with your friends again. However, make no mistake, things will have changed! Big time. You've not heard of the new bands or seen the new films, you don't know about the new bars and clubs, you haven't read any of the latest novels, and you've probably nothing much to talk about apart from your kids. Worst of all, your friends have started looking at you in a different way. To them, and astonishingly everyone else, your statement shirts have become dad shirts, your Saturday night club moves have become dad dancing, and your topical, funny quips have become...dad jokes!

Let's face it, dad jokes have a bad reputation. Punchlines are often met with moans and groans, raised eyebrows, rolling eyes, cringing faces, or cries of "cheesy" especially from any kids that hear them. With such a reputation as this, you would assume that dad jokes are just not funny. However, this is simply not true as this collection of groaners, one-liners, fun puns, and eye-rollers proves.

What are dad jokes?

So what exactly is a dad joke, why are they associated with dads in the first place and, if they are so bad, why are they so popular?

The first thing to say is that they are not jokes about dads, they are jokes told by dads and many see them as part of a father's role in the family. Dad jokes tend to be "wholesome", gentle, and sometimes lame one-liners with a predictable pun or play on words as the punchline, which allows dads to tell them around their kids. It is likely to be for this reason that the term itself is pejorative and the jokes are often described as lame and unfunny—so called anti-humor.

The other side of this particular coin is that maybe the unfunny joke is so bad...that it's good! This "violation of the norm" happens in all artforms. Take, for example, *The Room*, a 2003 film starring James Franco, generally regarded as the worst film ever made and dubbed "the Citizen Cane" of bad movies. Yet, it still plays to packed houses at midnight shows all over North America. What about the story of Florence Foster Jenkins, known as the world's worst singer whose tone-deaf voice was so beloved that she sold out Carnegie Hall in New York, or the popularity of the MOBA (Museum of Bad Art) galleries in Massachusetts?

It's a dad thing

Of course, there is no reason that mothers or women in general can't tell jokes, but in recent years, psychologists have investigated the phenomenon and linked the telling of these types of jokes with men because of their more teasing style of playing and joking with their children. Telling jokes that are so bad that their children roll their eyes or groan at them is a form of teasing, particularly when the joke is at the children's expense and, often, for the joke-teller's amusement.

Marc Hye-Knudsen, a humour researcher at Aarhus University in Denmark, believes that dad jokes are a modern and gentler version of the age old rough-and-tumble play that fathers have engaged in with their children since the dawn of time. The kind of play more associated with men than women. He suggests that this is good for children as it challenges their egos and their emotions, helping them to learn "impulse control" and "emotional regulation".

In 2023, The British Psychological Society joined in, suggesting that in regularly telling jokes that are so bad that it is embarrassing, dads are showing their children that "embarrassment is not lethal". This is particularly important for adolescents who are often anxious about getting embarrassed. Telling dad jokes will push children's limits as to how much embarrassment they can handle, helping them to overcome their fear of it.

That proves it then, dad jokes are officially and psychologically a good thing. So, what are you waiting for? It's time for you dads to partake in a proud tradition that is as old as time itself. Have a read through the 100s of groaners, one-liners, puns, and side-splitters contained in this wonderful volume of fun! Brush up on your joke-telling techniques and timing...and knock 'em out with your hilarious quips.

ONE-LINERS

If you see a robbery at an Apple store, does that make you an iWitness?

Where do you learn to make a banana split?

Sundae school.

Did you hear the one about the crustacean accused of promoting his own shellfish interests?

I used to hate facial hair... but then it grew on me.

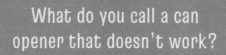

What do you call a can
opener that doesn't work?

A can't opener!

The wedding was so beautiful,
even the cake was in tiers.

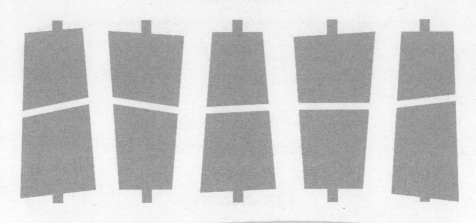

I tell dad jokes but I don't have any kids. I'm a faux pa!

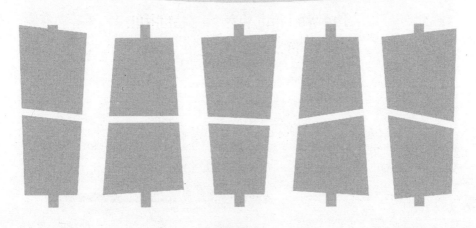

What do you call a factory that makes OK products?

A satisfactory.

How do you stop a bagel running away?

Put lox on it.

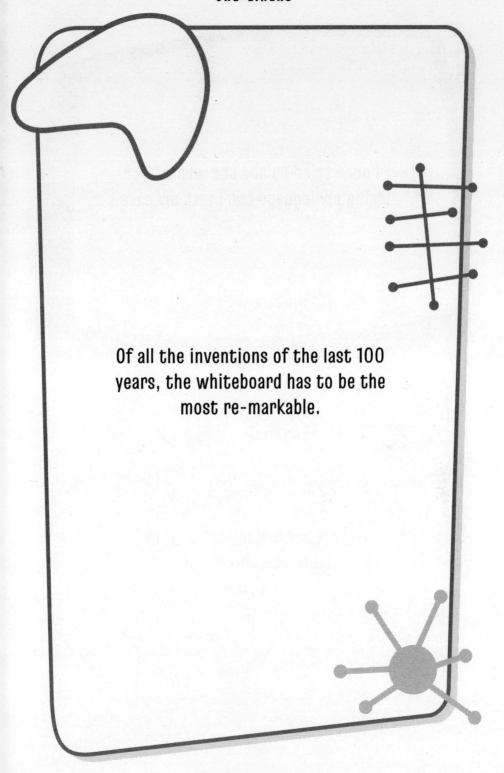

Of all the inventions of the last 100 years, the whiteboard has to be the most re-markable.

I once tried to sue the airport for losing my luggage but I lost my case.

People are making apocalypse jokes like there is no tomorrow!

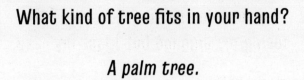

What kind of tree fits in your hand?

A palm tree.

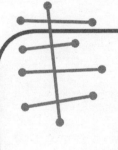

Guess who I bumped into
on my way to get my new
glasses?

Everybody!

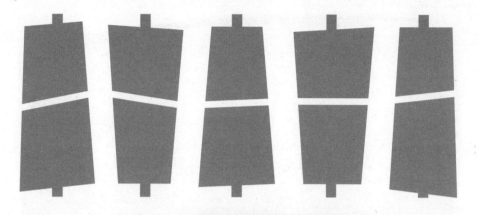

I just ordered the personal number plate BAA BAA.

Should look cool on my black jeep.

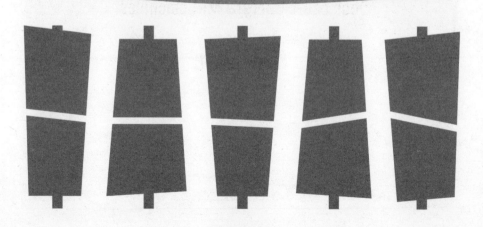

What's green with six legs and will
crush you if it falls on you?

A pool table.

Dogs can't operate MRI machines.

But catscan.

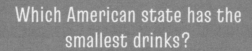

Which American state has the smallest drinks?

Mini-soda!

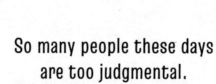

So many people these days are too judgmental.

I can tell just by looking at them.

When does a sandwich cook?

When it's bakin' lettuce and tomato.

What musical genre are
national anthems?

Country.

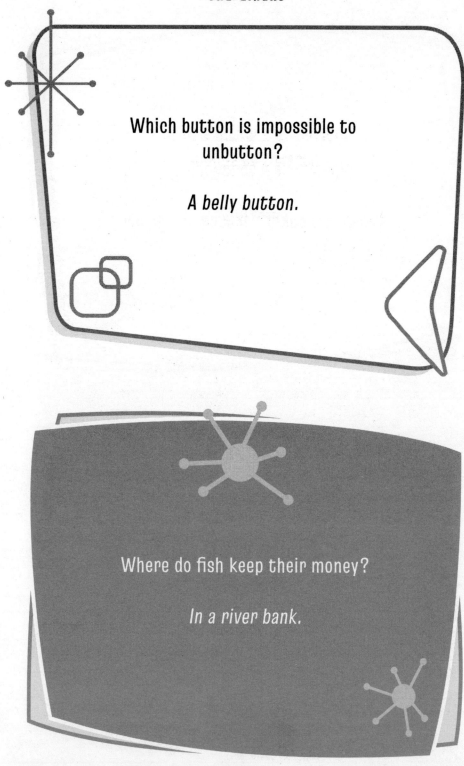

Which button is impossible to unbutton?

A belly button.

Where do fish keep their money?

In a river bank.

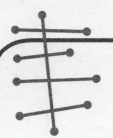

What is a witch's best
subject at school?

Spelling.

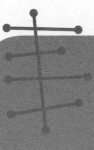

What do you call a rabbit
who got sunburn at Easter?

A hot-cross bunny.

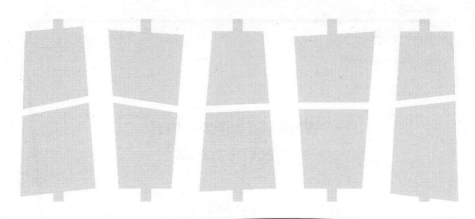

I used to run a dating service for chickens, but I was struggling to make hens meet!

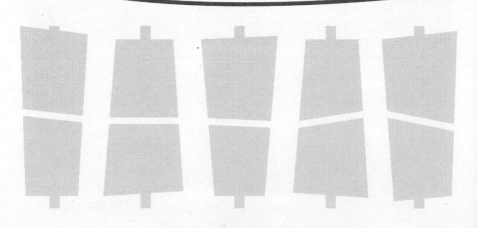

Why do gossips make terrible baristas?

They always spill the beans.

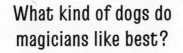

What kind of dogs do
magicians like best?

Labracadabradors.

How do you get a farm girl
to marry you?

First, a tractor.

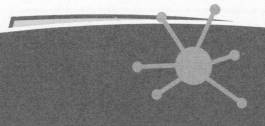

What's worse than finding a worm
in your apple?

Finding half a worm.

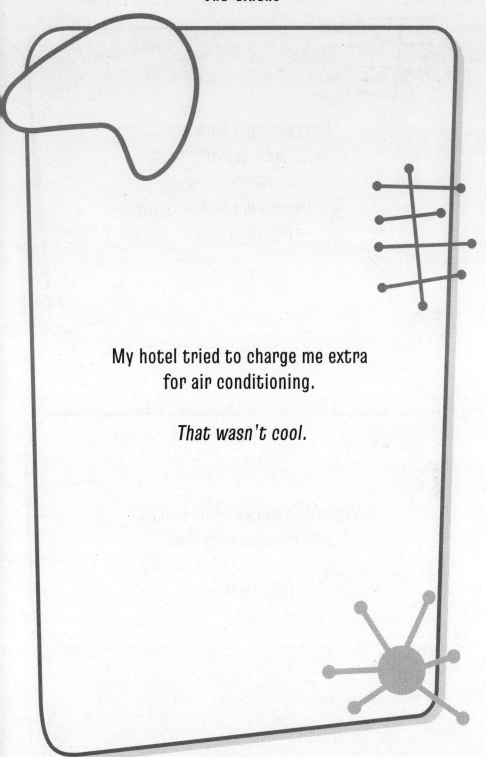

My hotel tried to charge me extra
for air conditioning.

That wasn't cool.

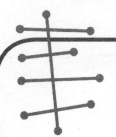

I'm reading a book about anti-gravity.

It's impossible to put down.

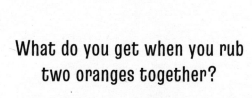

What do you get when you rub two oranges together?

Pulp friction.

What did the paper say to the pencil?

That's a good point.

Without geometry life is pointless.

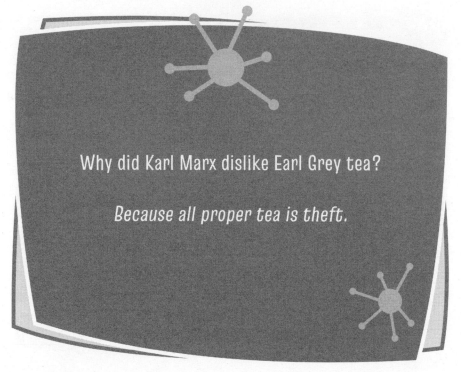

Why did Karl Marx dislike Earl Grey tea?

Because all proper tea is theft.

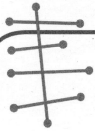

Why did Shakespeare's wife
leave him?

She got sick of all the drama.

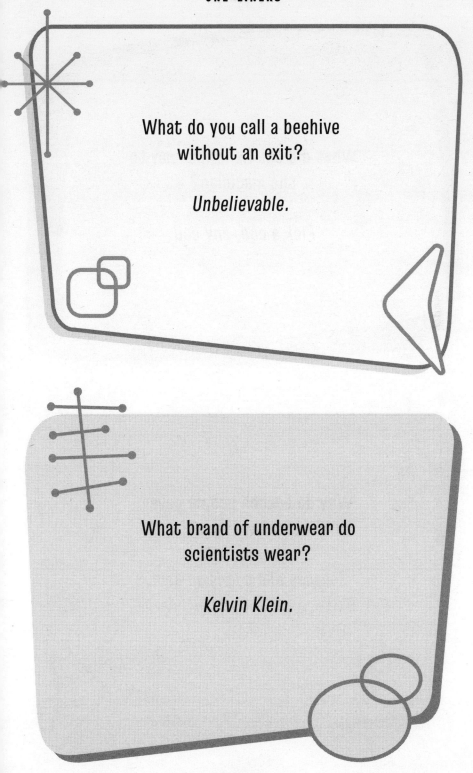

What do you call a beehive
without an exit?

Unbelievable.

What brand of underwear do
scientists wear?

Kelvin Klein.

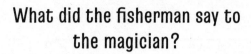

What did the fisherman say to
the magician?

Pick a cod, any cod.

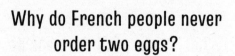

Why do French people never
order two eggs?

Because one egg is an oeuf.

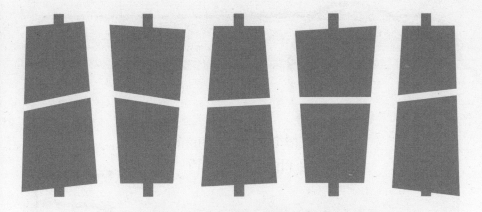

My wife asked if I had seen the dog bowl.

I said I didn't know he could.

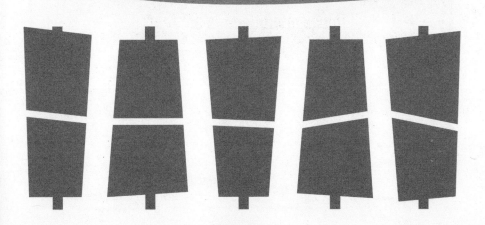

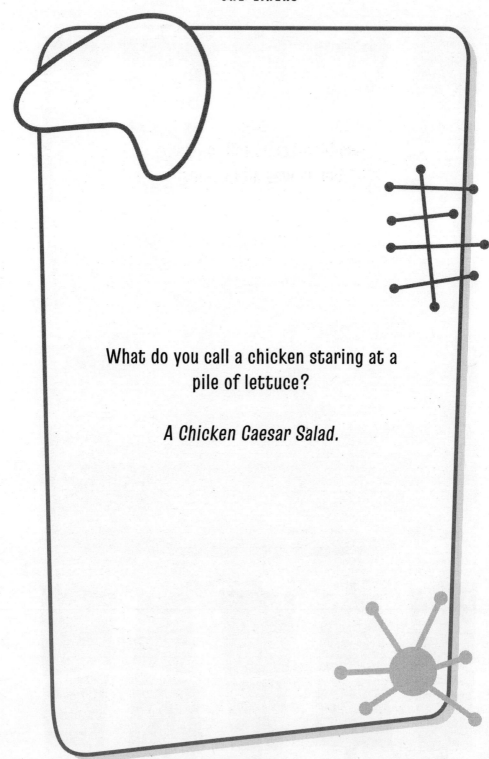

What do you call a chicken staring at a pile of lettuce?

A Chicken Caesar Salad.

Two blood cells fell in love...
but it was all in vein.

What do you call a baby ape?

A chimp off the old block.

Where do bad rainbows go?

Prism, but it's only a light sentence.

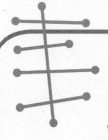

What do you get when you
ask a lemon for help?

Lemon aid.

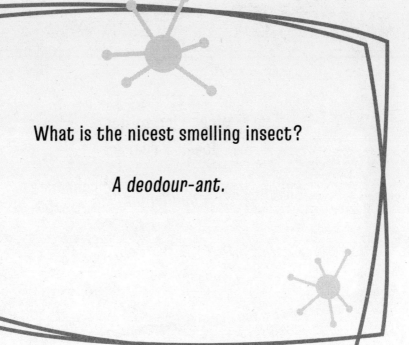

What is the nicest smelling insect?

A deodour-ant.

What's orange and sounds
like a parrot?

A carrot!

What kind of lion
doesn't roar?

A dandelion.

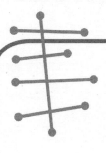

I've decided to get a pet
termite.

I'm going to call him Clint,
Clint Eatswood.

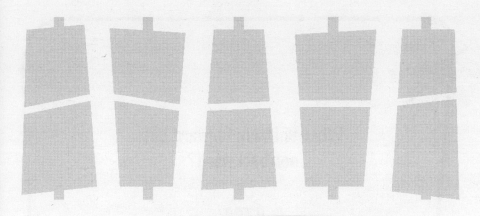

What musical instrument would you
find in the bathroom?

A tuba toothpaste.

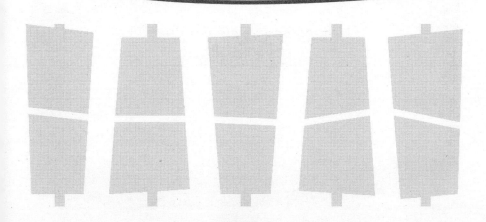

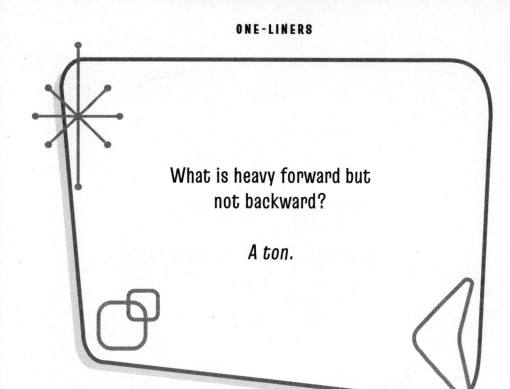

What is heavy forward but
not backward?

A ton.

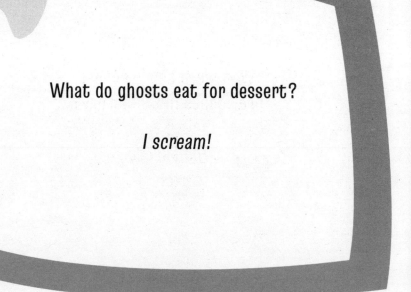

What do ghosts eat for dessert?

I scream!

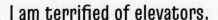

I am terrified of elevators.

I'm going to take steps to avoid them.

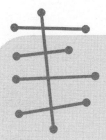

Who were the greenest
presidents in US history?

The bushes.

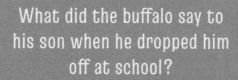

What did the buffalo say to
his son when he dropped him
off at school?

Bison.

The only thing that flat
earthers fear is sphere itself.

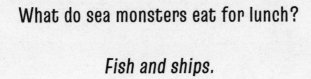

What do sea monsters eat for lunch?

Fish and ships.

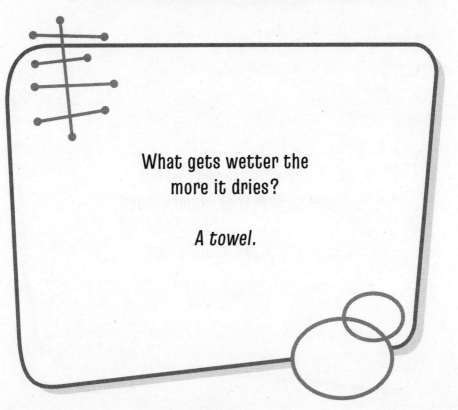

What gets wetter the
more it dries?

A towel.

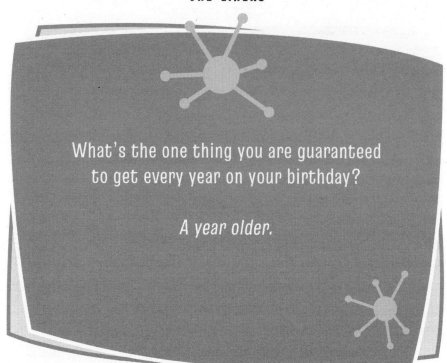

What's the one thing you are guaranteed
to get every year on your birthday?

A year older.

My therapist says I have a
preoccupation for revenge.

We'll see about that.

What do you call a bear with
no socks on?

Bare foot.

Why does a geologist hate his job?

He's taken for granite.

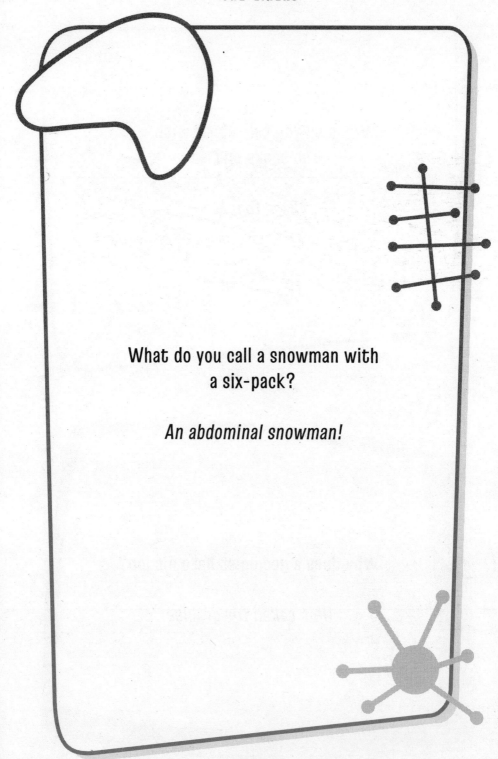

What do you call a snowman with
a six-pack?

An abdominal snowman!

People who use selfie sticks really need to have a good, long look at themselves.

What has hands but can't clap?

A clock.

What do you call a hippie's wife?

Mississippi.

What do you call a sleeping dinosaur?

A dino-SNORE.

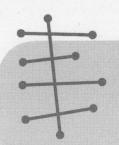

I start a new job in Seoul
next week.

*I hope it's going to be a good
Korea move.*

How do scientists freshen their breath?

With experi-mints.

What snacks do scholars eat?

Academia nuts.

Why do the French football team
keep scoring own goals?

Toulouse!

Who built King Arthur's round table?

Sir Cumference.

What did the clock do when
it was hungry?

It went back four seconds.

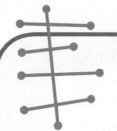

What did one wall say to
the other?

I'll meet you at the corner.

I've just eaten some bad seafood.

I'm feeling a little eel.

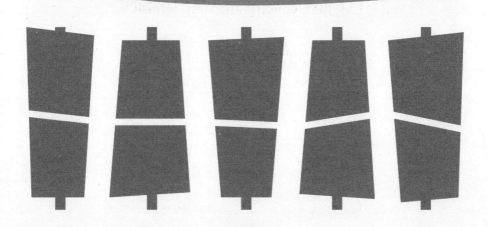

What do you call Santa's little helpers?

Subordinate clauses.

GROANERS AND EYE ROLLERS

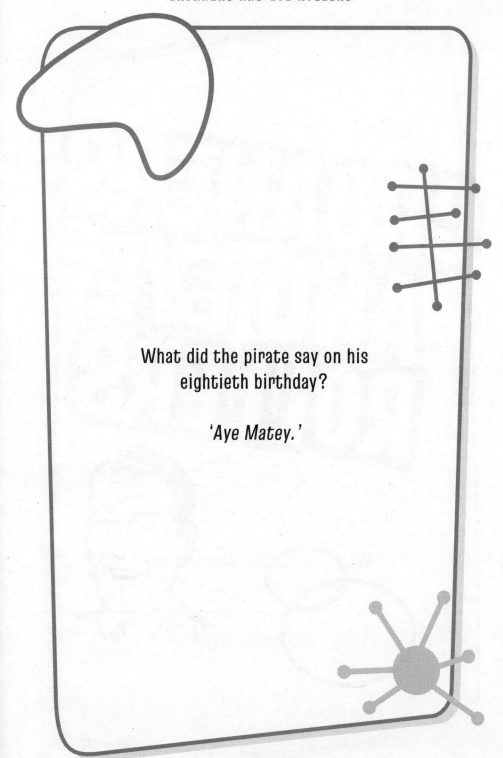

What did the pirate say on his
eightieth birthday?

'Aye Matey.'

What do you call a donkey
with three legs?

A wonkey.

What did the Zen Buddhist say
to the hotdog seller?

'Make me one with everything.'

What do you get if you cross
a snowman with a vampire?

Frostbite.

What do you call a female
magician in the desert?

A sand witch.

How do ghosts stay in shape?

They exorcise.

Last night I saw a documentary on how ships are put together.

It was riveting!

Two antennas met on a roof, fell in love, and got married.

The ceremony wasn't much, but the reception was excellent!

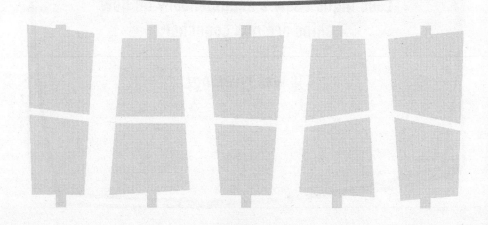

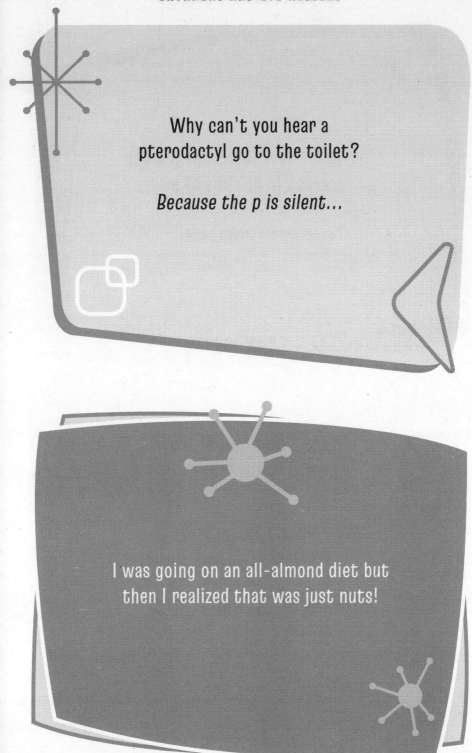

Why can't you hear a
pterodactyl go to the toilet?

Because the p is silent...

I was going on an all-almond diet but
then I realized that was just nuts!

The detectives found the murder
weapon in no time at all.

It was a briefcase.

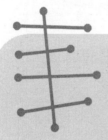

Why did the golfer bring two
pairs of socks?

In case he got a hole in one.

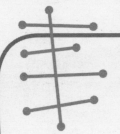

Why can't a nose be 12 inches long?

Because then it would be a foot.

What happens when a strawberry gets run over crossing the street?

Traffic jam!

What's the Easter Bunny's
music of choice?

Hip-hop.

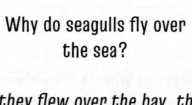

Why do seagulls fly over
the sea?

*If they flew over the bay, they
would be bagels.*

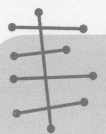

What do a tick and the Eiffel Tower have in common?

They're both Paris sites.

Why don't Italian restaurants serve spaghetti after 10pm.

It's pasta bedtime.

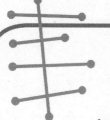

What would the Terminator
be called in his retirement?

The Exterminator.

My chemistry set blew up,
I guess oxidants happen.

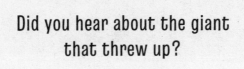

Did you hear about the giant
that threw up?

It's all over town!

Two goldfish are in a tank.

*One says to the other, "Do you know
how to drive this thing?"*

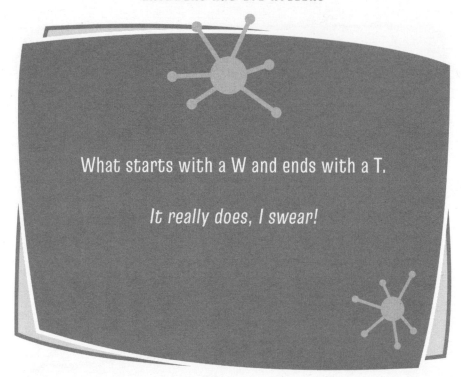

What starts with a W and ends with a T.

It really does, I swear!

I'm so good at sleeping I can do it with my eyes closed!

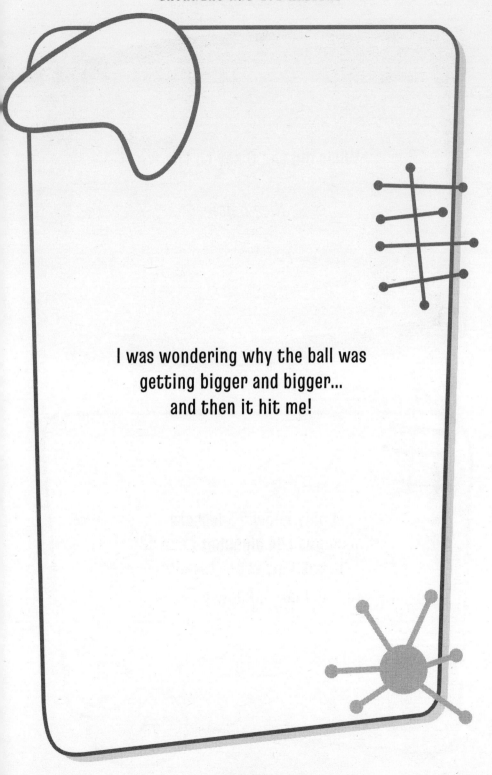

I was wondering why the ball was
getting bigger and bigger...
and then it hit me!

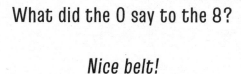

What did the 0 say to the 8?

Nice belt!

I only know 25 letters
of the alphabet.

I don't know y.

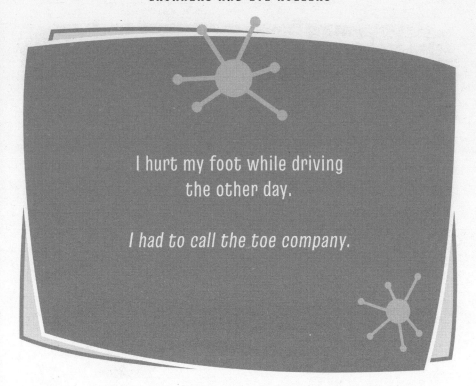

I hurt my foot while driving
the other day.

I had to call the toe company.

I'm afraid for the calendar.

Its days are numbered.

What's harder to catch
the faster you run?

Your breath!

Wanna hear a joke about a pizza?

Never mind, it's too cheesy.

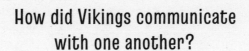

How did Vikings communicate
with one another?

By Norse code.

What do you call a magician
who lost their magic?

Ian.

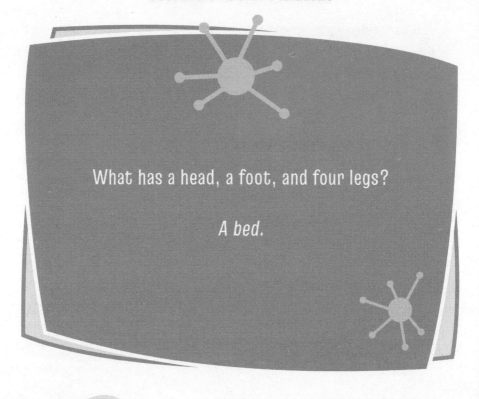

What has a head, a foot, and four legs?

A bed.

How can you tell when a
vampire is ill.

He can't stop coffin.

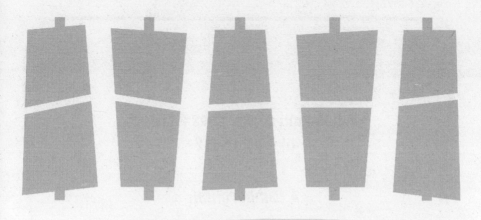

Singing in the shower is fun until you get soap in your mouth.

Then it's a soap opera.

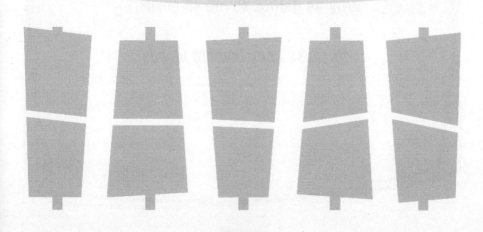

What kind of car does a sheep
like to drive?

A Lamborghini.

Why do giants sound so smart?

Because they use big words!

What kind of key opens the
door to a haunted house?

A spoo-key.

Last night I accidentally drank a
bottle of invisible ink.

*I'm in the hospital now,
waiting to be seen.*

My wife and I laugh at how competitive we are.

But I laugh more.

Did you hear about the cartoonist found dead at his home?

Details are sketchy

Why shouldn't you trust trees?

They might be shady.

Is there a hole in your shoe?

No... Then how'd you get your foot in it?

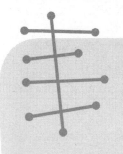

You can't trust atoms.

They make up everything!

What do you call an elephant that doesn't matter?

An irrelephant.

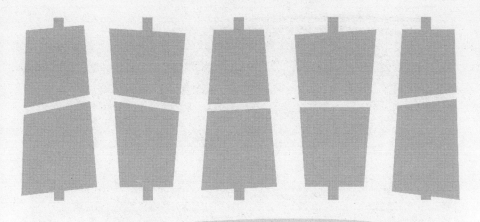

The three things I love most
are eating my family and not
using commas.

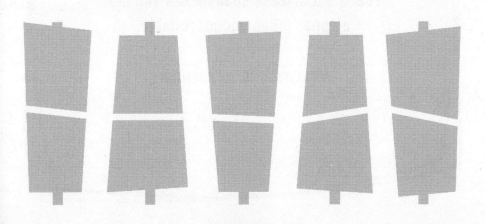

What's the loudest pet you can get?

A trumpet.

There's a disease that makes you tell airport jokes uncontrollably.

No cure... it's terminal.

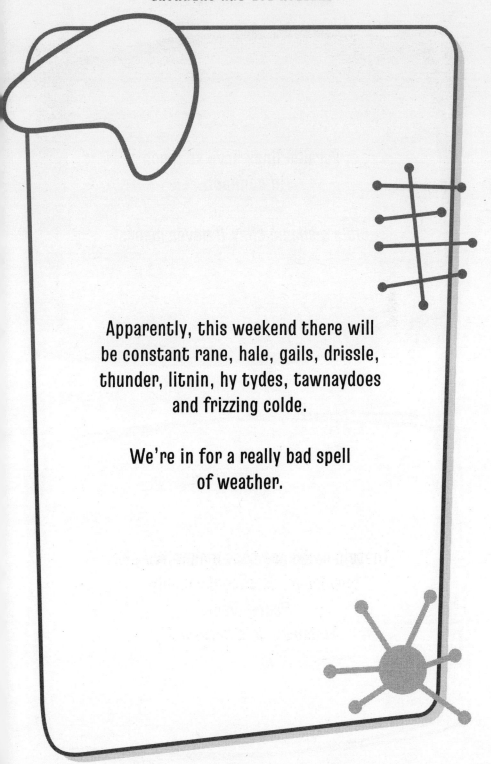

Apparently, this weekend there will
be constant rane, hale, gails, drissle,
thunder, litnin, hy tydes, tawnaydoes
and frizzing colde.

We're in for a really bad spell
of weather.

Parallel lines have so much in common.

It's a shame they'll never meet.

Where do pencils go on holiday?

Pencil-vania.

How does a penguin build a house?

Igloos it together.

What do frogs wear on their
feet in summer?

Open-toad sandals.

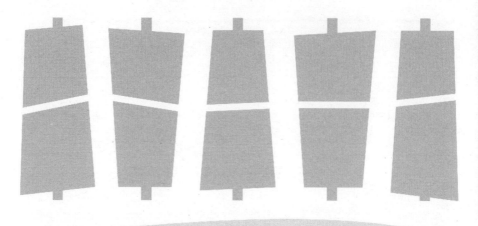

What's the difference between the
bird flu and the swine flu?

*One requires tweetment and the
other an oinkment.*

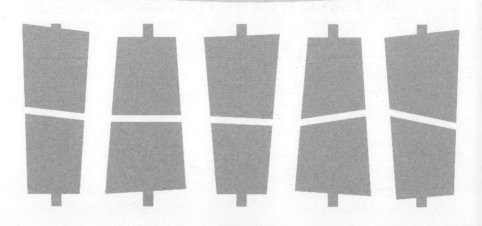

I don't trust stairs because they're always up to something.

Which animal is the most condescending?

A pan-duh!

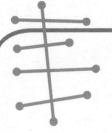

How do you tell the
difference between a dog
and tree?

By their bark.

What you call birds that stay
close together?

Velcrows.

Yesterday, a clown held a door
open for me.

I thought it was a nice jester.

I used to be addicted to the
hokey pokey, but I turned
myself around.

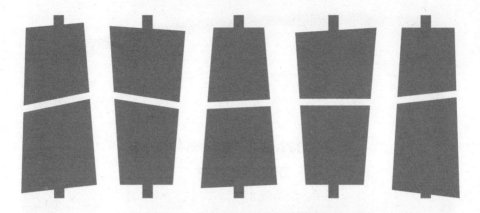

Sometimes I tuck my knees into my chest and lean forward.

That's just how I roll.

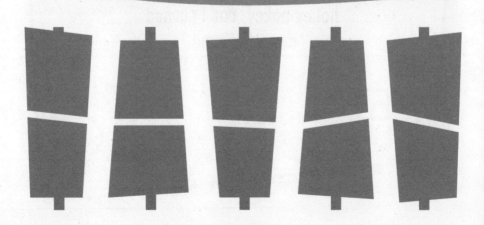

Why did the scarecrow win an award?

It was outstanding in its field.

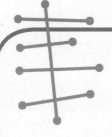

When does Friday come
before Thursday?

In the dictionary.

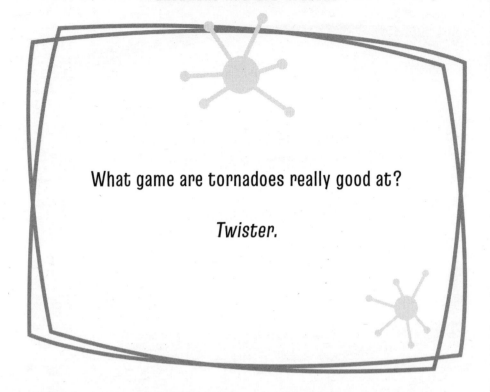

What game are tornadoes really good at?

Twister.

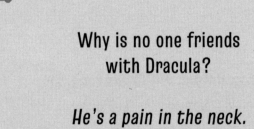

Why is no one friends
with Dracula?

He's a pain in the neck.

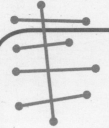

What kind of fish knows how
to do an appendectomy?

A Sturgeon.

What do you call a zen master
in charge of snacks?

A chipmunk.

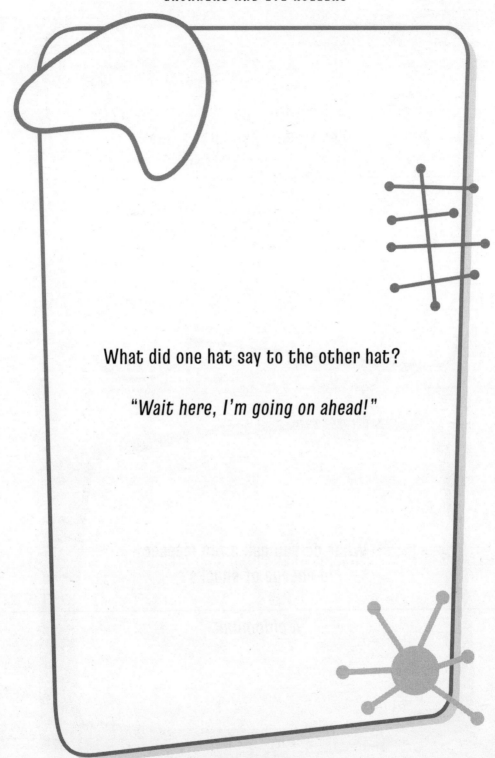

What did one hat say to the other hat?

"Wait here, I'm going on ahead!"

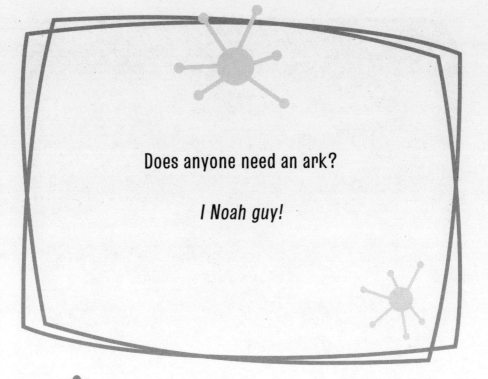

Does anyone need an ark?

I Noah guy!

I have a hen who regularly
counts her eggs.

She's a real mathamechicken.

How do cows stay
up-to-date?

They read the Moospaper.

Where are all the dad
jokes stored?

In a dad-a-base.

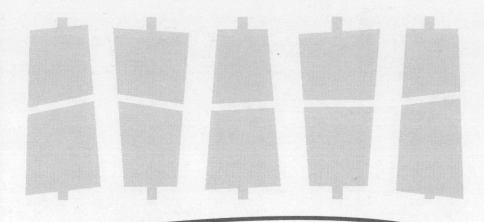

What item of clothing do clouds wear?

Thunderwear.

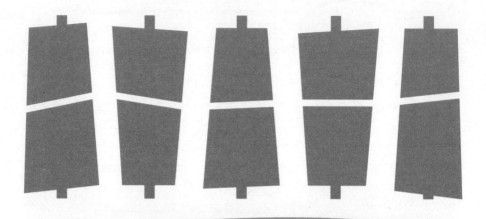

The past, present, and future walked
into a bar... it was tense!

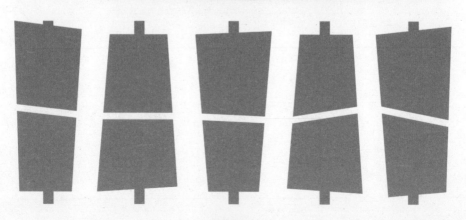

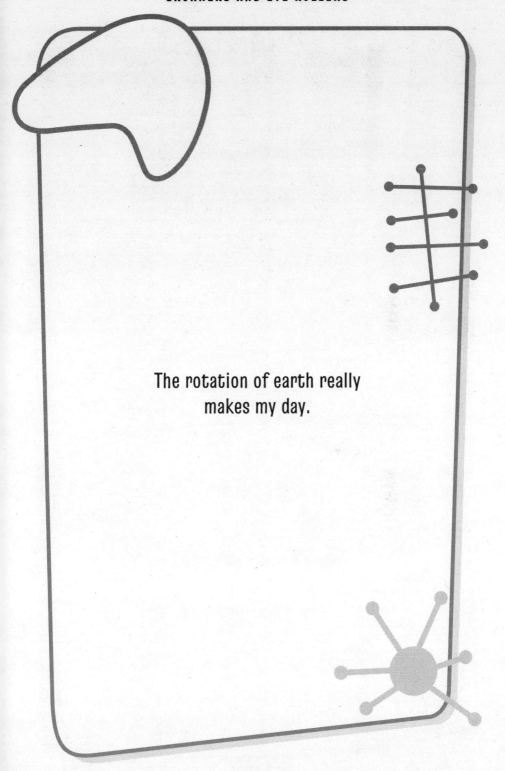

The rotation of earth really
makes my day.

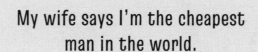

My wife says I'm the cheapest man in the world.

But I'm not buying it.

What's E.T. short for?

Because he's only got little legs!

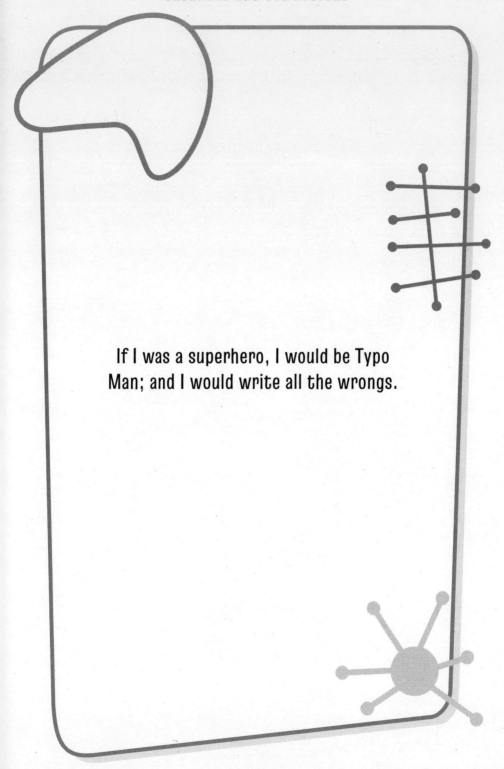

If I was a superhero, I would be Typo Man; and I would write all the wrongs.

Q: What did the alpaca say
to his date?

A: "Want to go on a picnic?
Alpaca lunch."

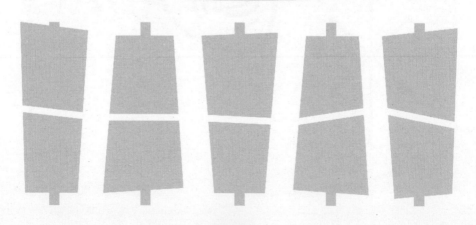

Q: Did you know milk is the fastest liquid on earth?

A: *It's pasteurized before you even see it.*

Q: What kind of music do the planets listen to?

A: *Nep-tunes!*

Q: Why did everyone enjoy being
around the volcano?

A: *It's just so lava-ble.*

Q: What did the big flower say
to the tiny flower?

A: *"Hey there bud!"*

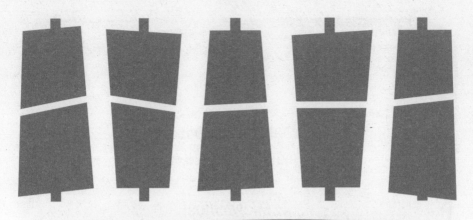

Q: What do you call Chewbacca when
he has chocolate stuck in his fur?

A: A chocolate chip Wookie.

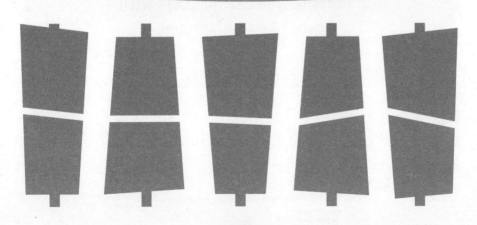

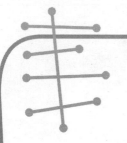

Q: What's a computer's
snack of choice?

A: *Microchips!*

Q: What do you call monkeys with a
shared Amazon account?

A: *Prime mates.*

Q: What do you call your grandma's
number on speed dial?

A: Instagran.

Q: What's worse than raining
cats and dogs?

A: Hailing taxis.

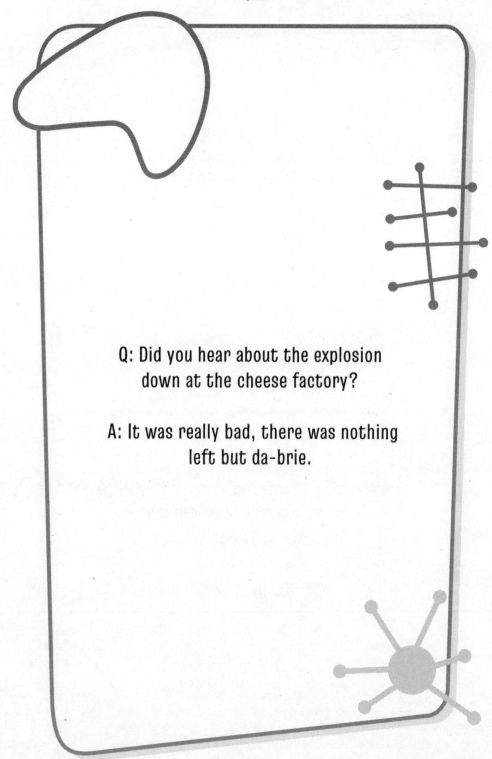

Q: Did you hear about the explosion
down at the cheese factory?

A: It was really bad, there was nothing
left but da-brie.

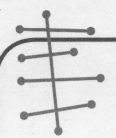

Q: Why was the smartphone's
camera blurry?

A: *It had lost its contacts.*

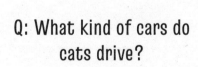

Q: What kind of cars do
cats drive?

A: *Catillacs.*

Q: When does a joke become a
dad joke?

A: *When it's fully groan...*

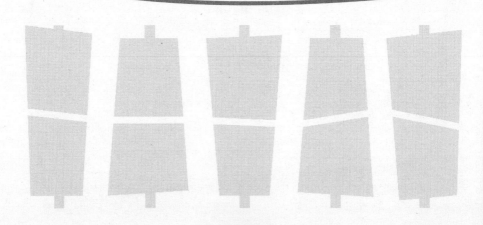

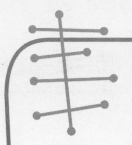

Q: What happened when
the man crashed his
expensive car?

A: *He found out how a
Mercedes bends.*

Q: What do you get when you put
a car and a pet together?

A: *A carpet.*

Q: What do you call a knight made entirely out of fine china?

A: *Sir Ramic*

Q: What do you call a row of people lifting mozzarella?

A: *A cheesy pick-up line.*

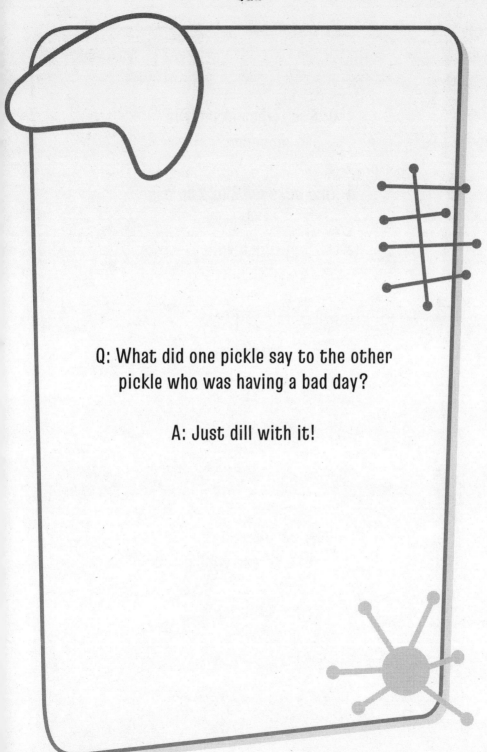

Q: What did one pickle say to the other
pickle who was having a bad day?

A: Just dill with it!

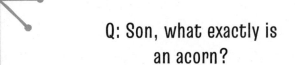

Q: Son, what exactly is an acorn?

A: *In a nutshell? It's an oak tree.*

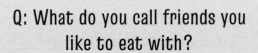

Q: What do you call friends you like to eat with?

A: *Taste buds.*

Q: What's green and loves the snow?

A: A skiwi!

Q: Why you should never tell secrets to pigs?

A: They're always the first to squeal.

Q: What happened to the guy who lit
a fire in his canoe to keep warm?

A: *He learned that you can't have your
kayak and heat it too.*

Q: How do fleas like to travel?

A: *They prefer to itch hike.*

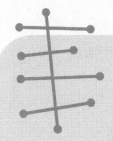

Q: Why do basketball players always have dirty shirts?

A: *They are famous for their dribbling.*

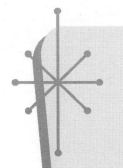

Q: What did the proton say to the neutron?

A: *Stop being so negative!*

Q: What's the coolest scientific discipline?

A: *Geology, because it totally rocks!*

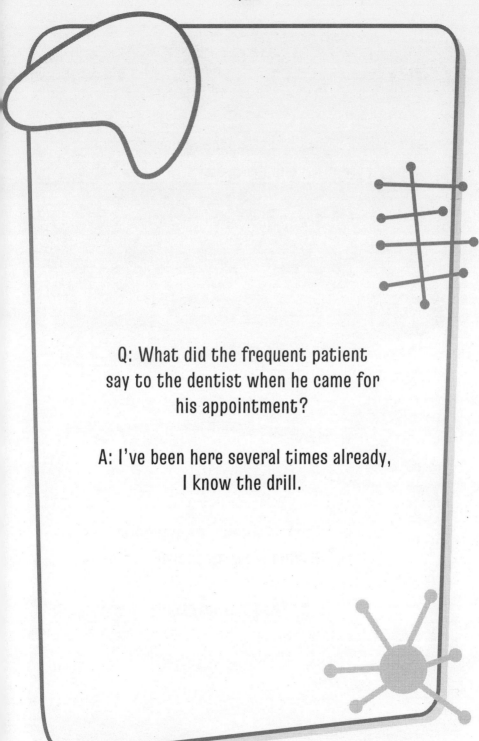

Q: What did the frequent patient
say to the dentist when he came for
his appointment?

A: I've been here several times already,
I know the drill.

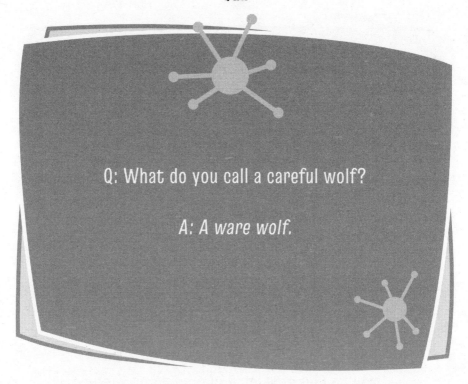

Q: What do you call a careful wolf?

A: *A ware wolf.*

Q: Which dinosaur is known for
having amazing teeth?

A: *The Flossoraptor!*

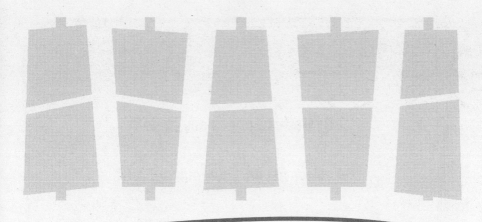

Q: How many tickles does it take to
make an octopus laugh?

A: *Ten tickles.*

Q: How do poets say hello?

A: *Hey, haven't we metaphor?*

Q: What kind of business would Yoda start?

A: *A Toy Yoda dealership*

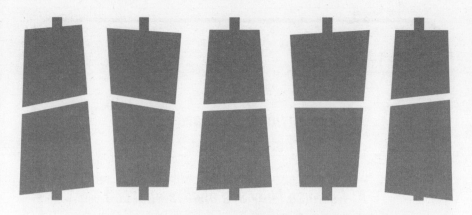

Q: What's the difference between
Black Eyed Peas and chickpeas?

A: *Black Eyed Peas can sing us a song.
Chickpeas can only hummus one.*

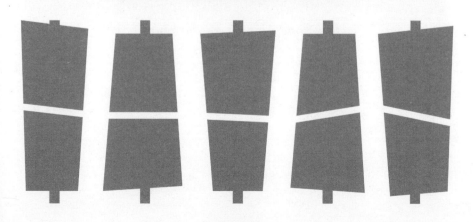

Q: Why can't leopards play
hide-and-seek?

A: *Because they are always spotted.*

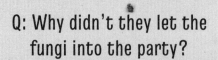

Q: Why didn't they let the
fungi into the party?

A: *There wasn't mush room.*

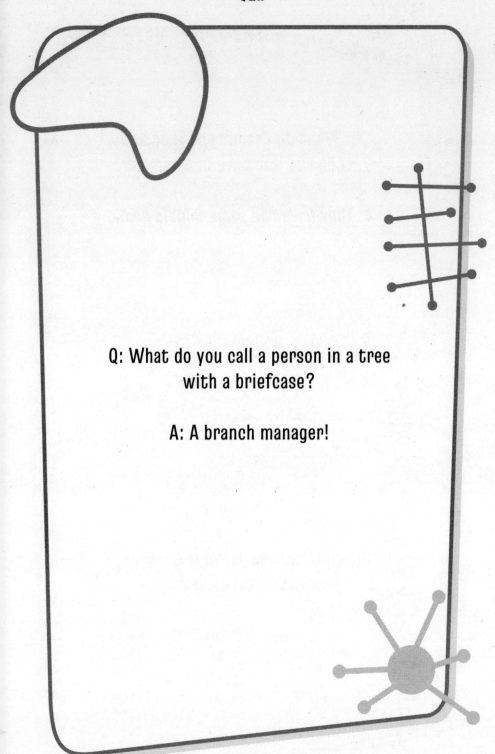

Q: What do you call a person in a tree with a briefcase?

A: A branch manager!

Q: What do Kermit the Frog and Attila the Hun have in common?

A: *They have the same middle name.*

Q: Which dinosaur had the most impressive vocabulary?

A: *The thesaurus.*

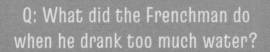

Q: What did the Frenchman do
when he drank too much water?

A: *He went oui oui in
his trousers.*

Q: Which Star Wars
character works at
a restaurant?

A: *Darth Waiter!*

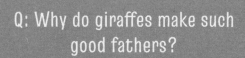

Q: Why do giraffes make such
good fathers?

A: *Because they're easy to look up to.*

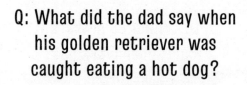

Q: What did the dad say when
his golden retriever was
caught eating a hot dog?

A: *"It's a dog-eat-dog world
out there."*

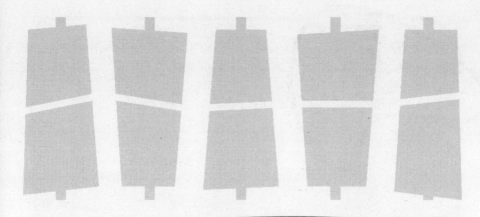

Q: How come the Hulk doesn't lose his trousers when he transforms?

A: *The experiment altered his genes.*

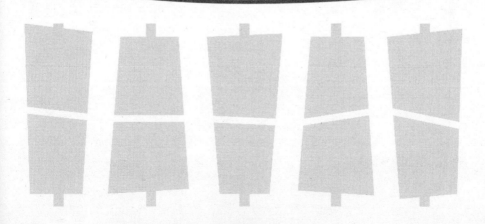

Q: What tone does a piano falling down a mineshaft make?

A: *A-flat minor.*

Q: You've heard of Pop-Tarts, right?
Why aren't there any Mom Tarts?

A: *It's because of the pastry-archy.*

Q: What did the flip-flops say to the
tennis shoes?

A: *Quit sneaking around!*

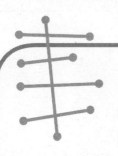

Q: What's the difference between an owl, a piano, and a fish?

A: *You can tune a piano, but you can't tuna fish. What about the owl, you say? Whoo?*

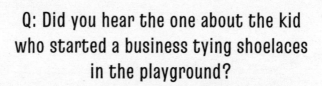

Q: Did you hear the one about the kid who started a business tying shoelaces in the playground?

A: *It was a knot-for-profit business.*

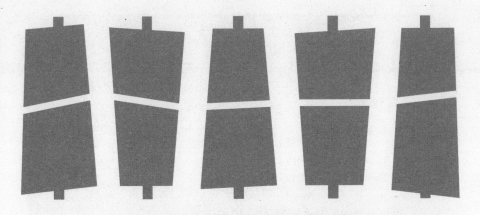

Q: What do you call two witches who live together?

Q: Broom mates.

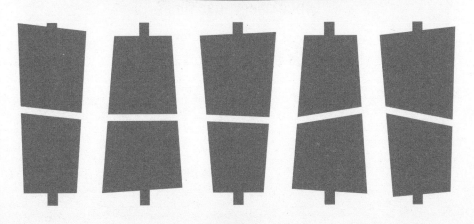

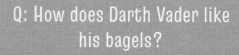

Q: How does Darth Vader like
his bagels?

A: *On the dark side.*

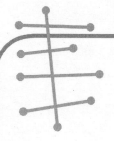

Q: Did you hear about
the man who fell into an
upholstery machine?

A: *He's fully re-covered.*

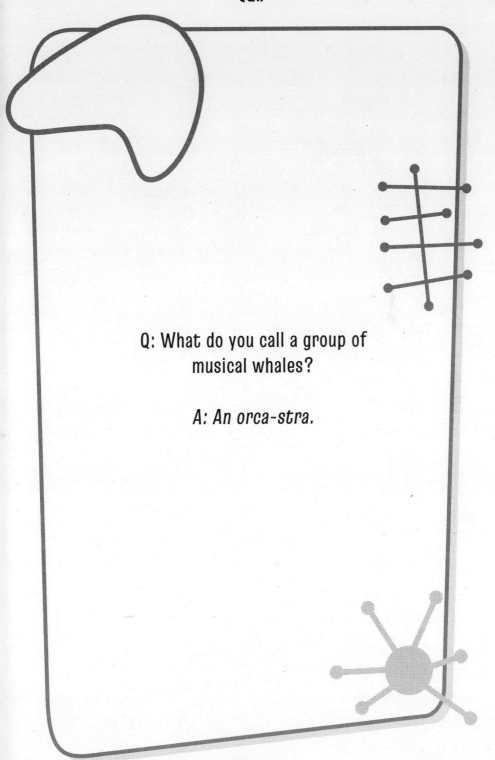

Q: What do you call a group of
musical whales?

A: *An orca-stra.*

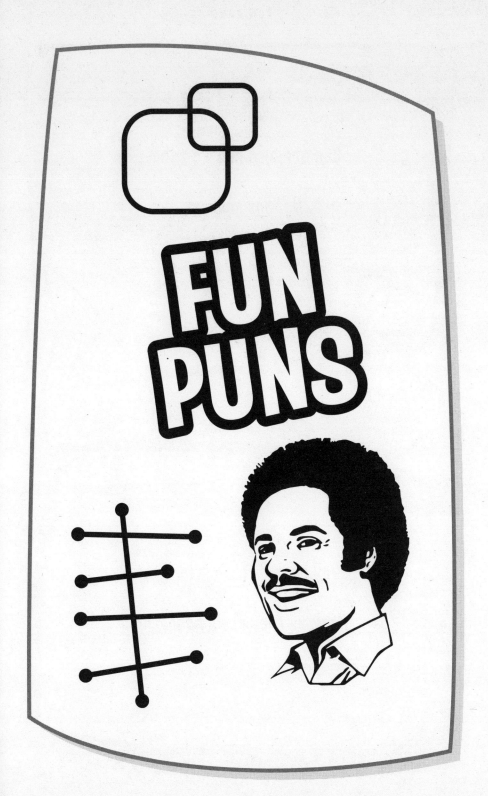

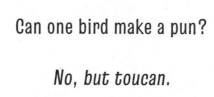

Can one bird make a pun?

No, but toucan.

Why do bees have sticky hair?

Because they use a honeycomb.

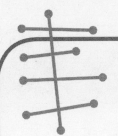

Justice is a dish best
served cold.

*If it were served warm,
it would be just-water.*

I'm addicted to seaweed.

I must seek kelp!

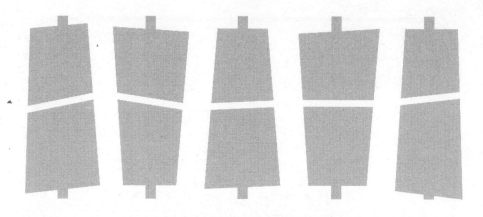

My wife asked me the other day why I always had so many sweets.

I replied, "I always like to have a few Twix up my sleeve."

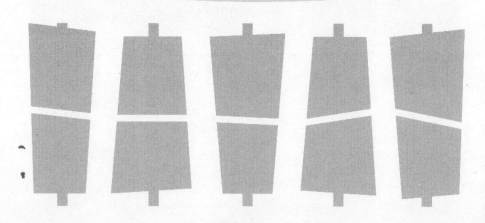

Cosmetic surgery used to be such a taboo subject.

Now you can talk about Botox and nobody raises an eyebrow.

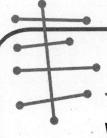

What do you call a dinosaur that asks a lot of deep questions?

A philosiraptor.

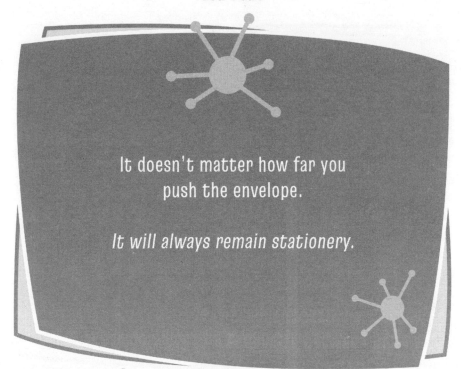

It doesn't matter how far you push the envelope.

It will always remain stationery.

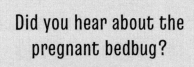

Did you hear about the pregnant bedbug?

She's due in the spring.

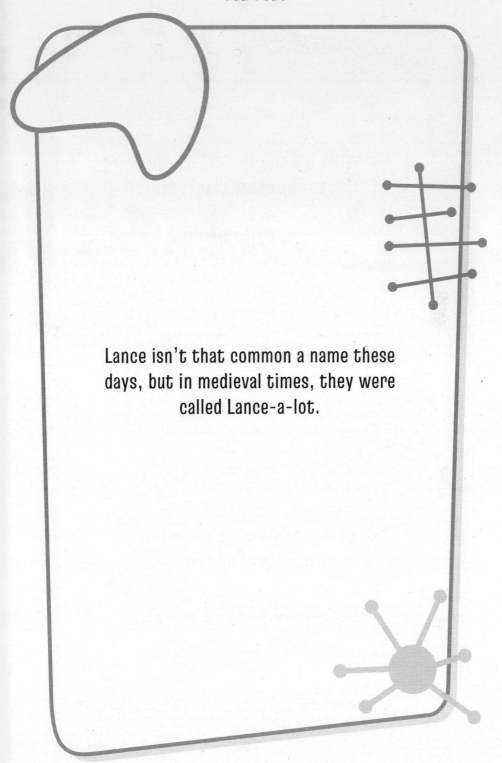

Lance isn't that common a name these days, but in medieval times, they were called Lance-a-lot.

What did the sick chickpea say
to the other chickpea

I falafel!

I accidentally handed my wife a
glue stick instead of chapstick.

She still isn't talking to me.

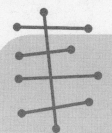

What's the difference between a clown and an athletic rabbit?

One is a bit funny and the other is a fit bunny.

I saw a man that used different cuts of steak to create portraits of people.

It was a rare medium, but well done!

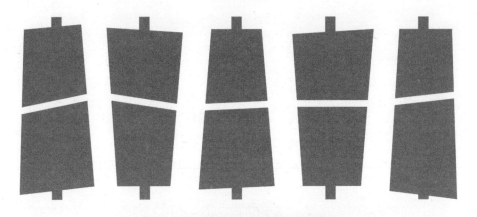

Word of a food shortage at this
year's spoonerism conference turned
out to be a complete lack of pies.

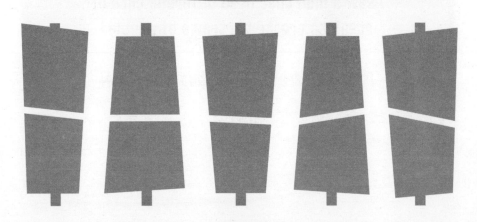

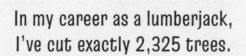

In my career as a lumberjack,
I've cut exactly 2,325 trees.

*Every time I chop one down,
I keep a log.*

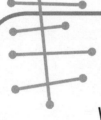

Why is it difficult to explain
puns to kleptomaniacs?

*Because they always take
things literally.*

The CEO of Ikea was appointed
Prime Minister of Sweden.

*He's currently assembling
his cabinet.*

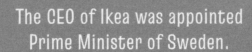

My wife yelled at me for having
no sense of direction.

*So I packed up my stuff
and right!*

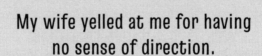

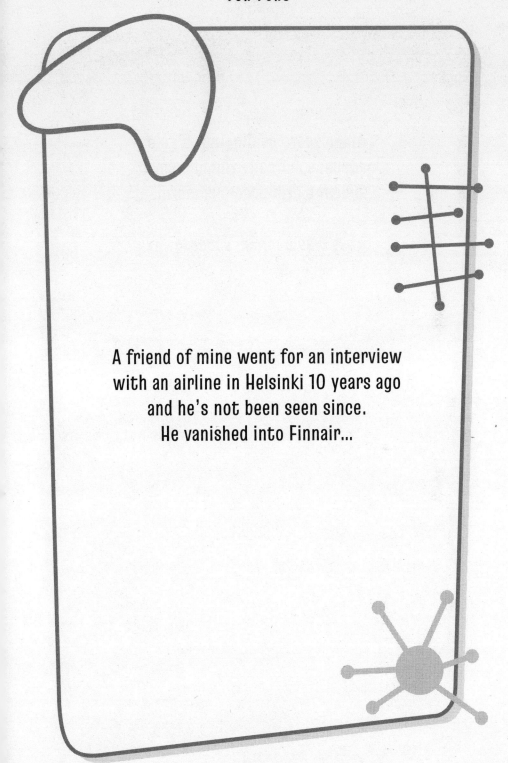

A friend of mine went for an interview
with an airline in Helsinki 10 years ago
and he's not been seen since.
He vanished into Finnair...

After years of digging, a gold prospector finally found a small amount of a precious metal.

It was a miner success.

The sea cucumber turned to the octopus and the sea urchin and said: "With friends like these, who needs anemones?"

My teacher asked me, "What's the difference between ignorance and apathy?"

I replied, "I don't know and I don't care!"

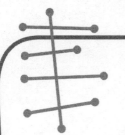

What word becomes shorter
when you add two letters?

Short.

Why do all witches wear black?

So you can't tell which witch is which!

What do dentists call X-rays?

Tooth pics!

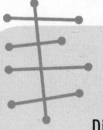

Did you hear about the nurse who didn't want to become a doctor?

She didn't have the patients.

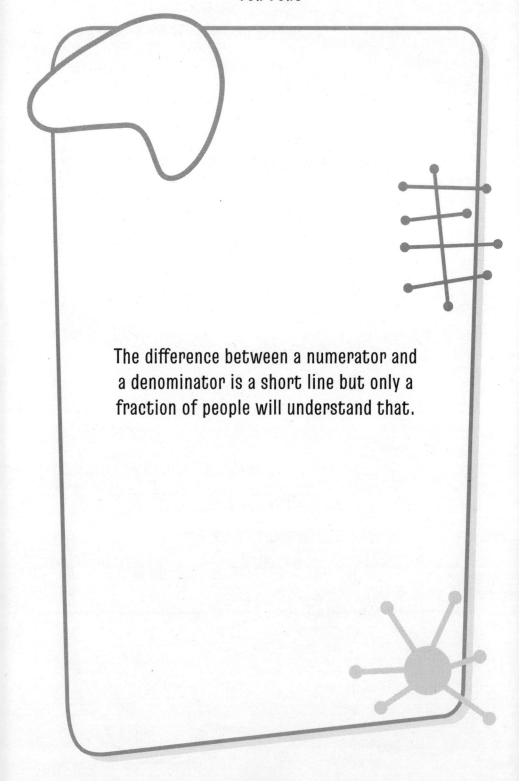

The difference between a numerator and a denominator is a short line but only a fraction of people will understand that.

What did the drummer dad
name his twin daughters?

Anna one, Anna two...

I'd tell you a chemistry joke but I
know I wouldn't get a reaction.

My friend keeps saying "cheer up, it could be worse. You could be stuck underground in a hole full of water."

I know he means well.

Ants are amazing creatures. Did you know viruses can't spread throughout an ant colony?

It's because of all the little anty bodies.

Which athletes are the warmest during winter competitions?

The long jumpers.

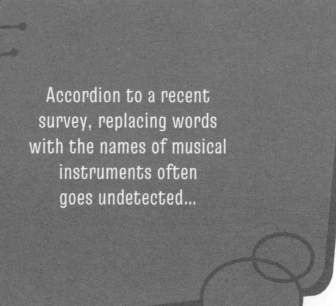

Accordion to a recent survey, replacing words with the names of musical instruments often goes undetected...

Last year I made loads of money clearing leaves from gardens.

I was raking it in.

I got a new pair of gloves today, but they're both lefts.

On the one hand, is great, but on the other, it's just not right.

I invented a new word today...
plagiarism!

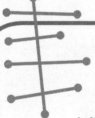

Why did the art thief's getaway
vehicle run out of fuel?

*Because he had no Monet to buy
Degas to make the Van Gogh!*

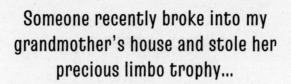

Someone recently broke into my grandmother's house and stole her precious limbo trophy...

How low can you go?

Did you hear about the antiques collector who found an old Coca-Cola lamp?

She was soda lighted.

Which website did
Chewbacca create?

Wookieleaks!

On our way home my other
half said let's stop and visit
our son Nicholas, so we took
the see Nick route!

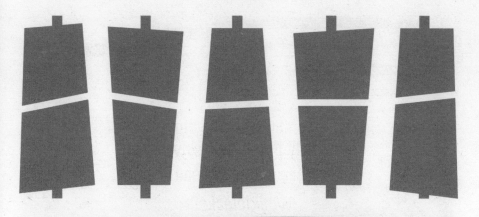

The other day I bought a thesaurus, but when I got home and opened it, all the pages were blank... I have no words to describe how angry I am.

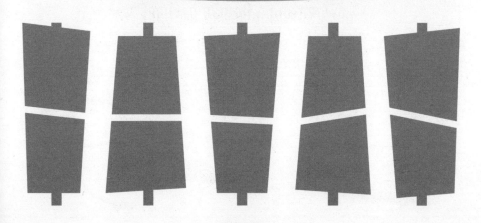

Recently I've taken to wearing
bread on my head.

It's a new loaf hat diet.

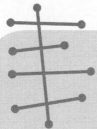

What is the difference
between an angry circus
owner and a Roman barber?

*One is a raving showman, the
other is a shaving roman.*

What do you call a locomotive
carrying bubble gum?

A chew chew train.

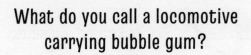

I only seem to be ill on weekdays.

I must have a weekend immune system.

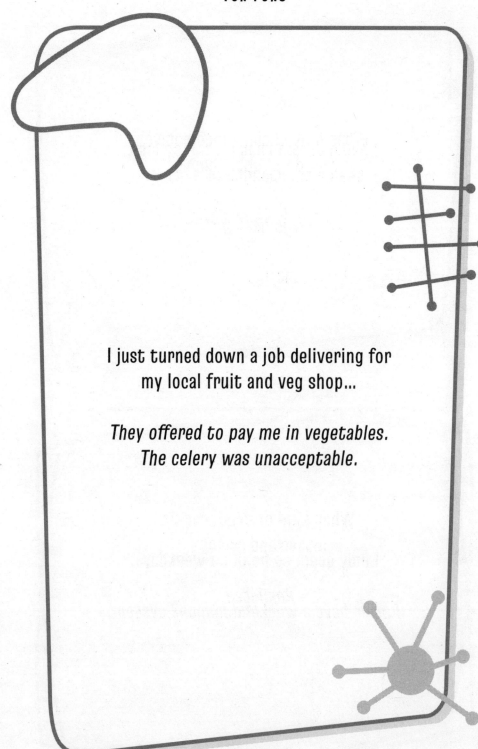

I just turned down a job delivering for
my local fruit and veg shop...

They offered to pay me in vegetables.
The celery was unacceptable.

I had a dream that I weighed less
than a thousandth of a gram.

I was like, Omg.

What kind of drink can be
bitter and sweet?

Reali-tea.

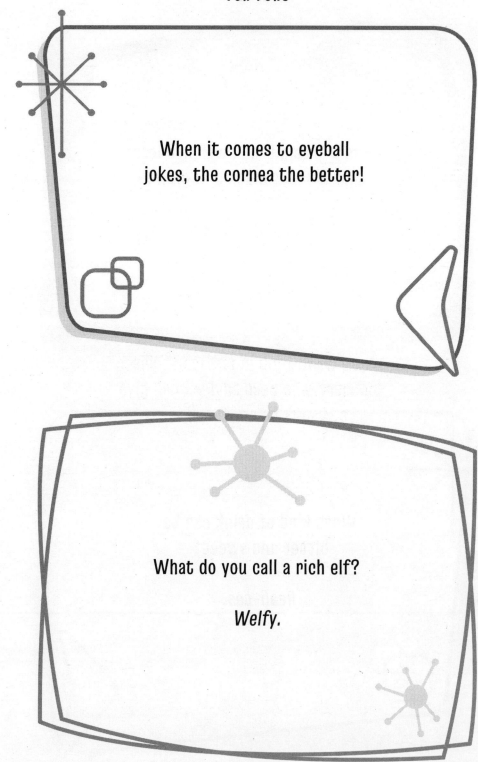

When it comes to eyeball jokes, the cornea the better!

What do you call a rich elf?

Welfy.

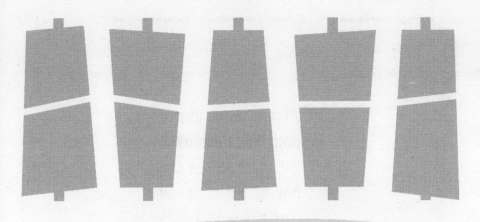

If you want a job in the moisturiser industry, the best advice I can give you is to apply daily.

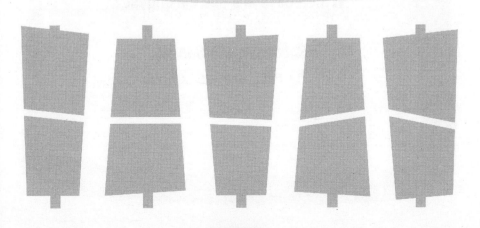

I don't know what the word
apocalypse means.

*But hey, it's not the end
of the world.*

Which days are the strongest?

*Saturday and Sunday.
The rest are weekdays.*

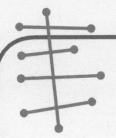

Be kind to dentists.

*They have fillings too,
you know.*

What happens to Nitrogen
when the sun rises?

It becomes Daytrogen.

A slice of apple pie is $2.50 in Jamaica and $3 in the Bahamas...

There are the pie rates of the Caribbean.

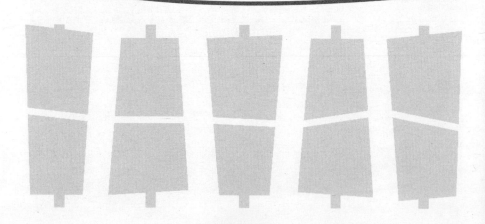

Which vegetables do plumbers like least?

Leeks.

What's the opposite of irony?

Wrinkly.

My friend really changed once she became a vegetarian.

It's like I've never seen herbivore.

I'm going to stand outside.

So if anyone asks, I'm outstanding.

What's the difference between a well-dressed man on a unicycle and a poorly dressed man on a bicycle?

Attire.

What do you call a carnivorous
weather forecaster?

A meat-eater-ologist.

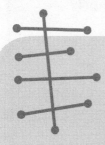

I used to work as a programmer
for autocorrect... but they fried
me for no raisin!

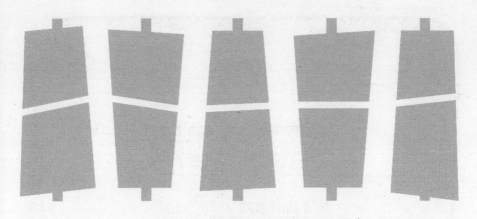

My housemate recently got really into
tropical food diet and now our house
is full of the stuff.

It's enough to make a mango crazy.

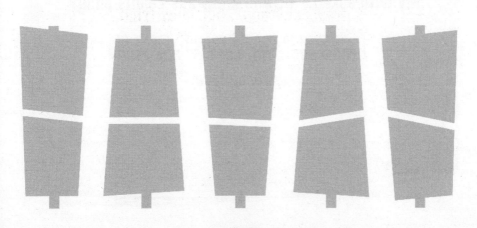

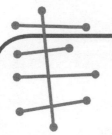

Apparently, you can't use
beef stew as a password.

It's just not stroganoff.

My wife asked, "Do you know any tennis puns?"

*I returned, "No, they're not really
my forte love."*

Becoming vegetarian was a huge missed steak.

Did you hear the one about the baguette at the zoo?

It was bread in captivity.

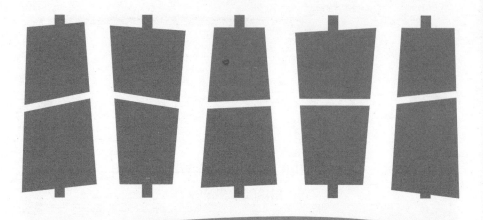

I can't decide if I want to pursue a career as a writer or a petty criminal.

I'm still weighing up the pros and cons.

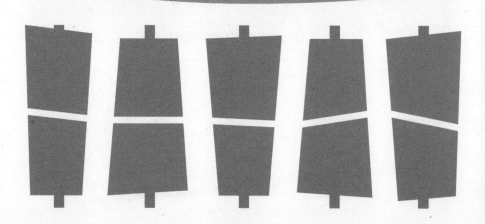

I went into a pet shop and asked for twelve bees. The shopkeeper counted out thirteen and handed them over. I said, "You've given me one too many".

He pointed at the last one and said, "That. That one's a free bee."

MISCELLANY

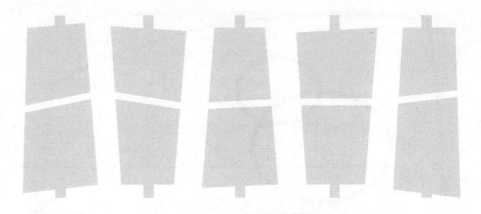

A man walks into a bookshop. He says
to the assistant, "Do you have any
books on turtles?"
She replies, "Hard back?"

*"Yes," says the customer,
"and little heads."*

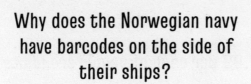

Why does the Norwegian navy have barcodes on the side of their ships?

So they can Scandinavian.

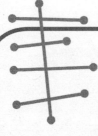

I've started telling everyone about the benefits of eating dried grapes... It's all about raisin awareness!

99.99 per cent of people are idiots.

I'm just happy that I belong to the 1 per cent.

What happens when a frog's car dies?

He needs a jump. If that doesn't work he has to get it toad.

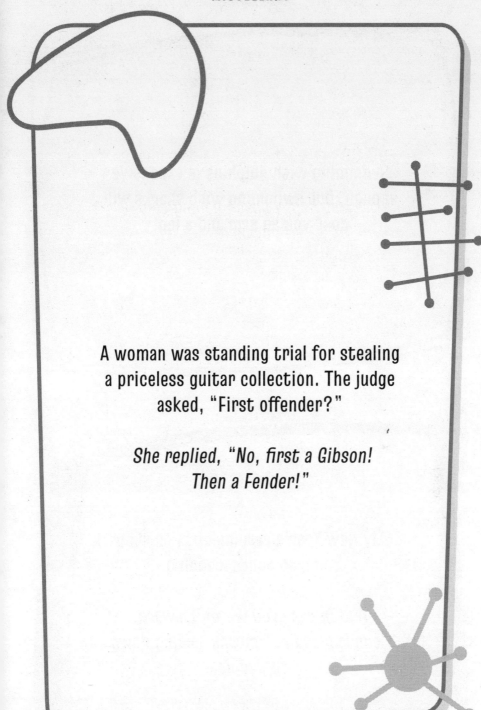

A woman was standing trial for stealing a priceless guitar collection. The judge asked, "First offender?"

She replied, "No, first a Gibson! Then a Fender!"

Swimming with dolphins is expensive enough, but swimming with sharks will cost you an arm and a leg!

My New Year's resolution is to stop being so condescending.

And in case you weren't aware, "condescending" means talking down to people.

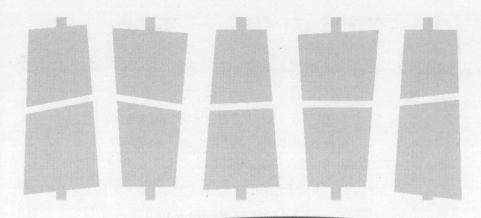

My friend asked me if I wanted to
hear a really good Batman impression,
so I said go on then. He shouted,
"NO, NOT THE KRYPTONITE!"

I said, "That's Superman..."
"Thanks," he replied, "I've been
working on it a lot."

I went to see the doctor about my blocked ear. "Which ear is it?" he asked.

"2024", I replied.

I was going to tell my kids a joke about Sodium, but then I thought, Na.

I asked the librarian if she had a
book about Pavlov's dog and
Schrödinger's cat.

*She said it rang a bell but she wasn't
sure if it was there or not.*

I once went to see a Mexican magician. He said he would disappear on the count of 3, "uno, dos..." poof.

He disappeared without a tres.

I'm Buzz Aldrin, second man to step on the moon.

Neil before me.

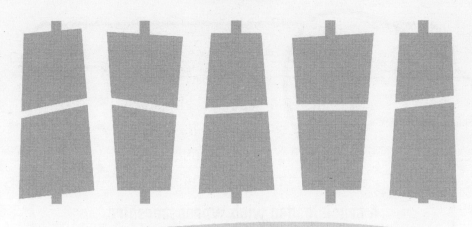

I met some chess players in the hotel lobby. They were bragging about how good they were.

They were chess nuts boasting in an open foyer.

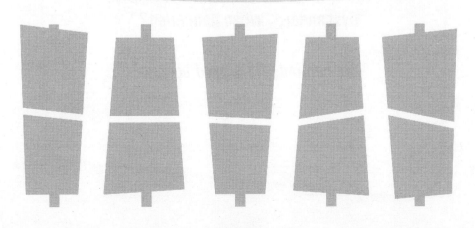

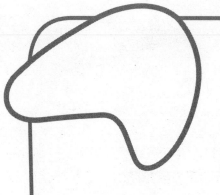

A truck loaded with Worcestershire sauce was driving through the Welsh town of Llanfairpwllgwyngyll in Anglesey on its way to Rhosllanerchrugog in Wrexham, when it collided with a Nissan Qashqai. The truck skidded down the road and hit a car from Llanfihangel Tre'r Beirdd, injuring the two otolaryngologists inside. One of them, suffering from schistosomiasis, had a myocardial infarction. A bystander witnessed the entire event and quickly called to report the accident. The emergency operator asked the bystander, "What happened?"

He replied, "It's hard to say."

Gravity is one of the most fundamental forces in the universe, but if you remove it, you get…. Gravy!

How many narcissists does it take to change a light bulb?

One. The narcissist holds the light bulb while the rest of the world revolves around him.

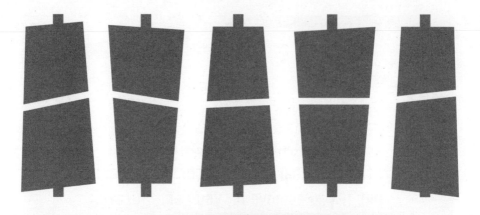

I was in a job interview the other day and they asked if I could perform under pressure.

I said no, but I could perform Bohemian Rhapsody.

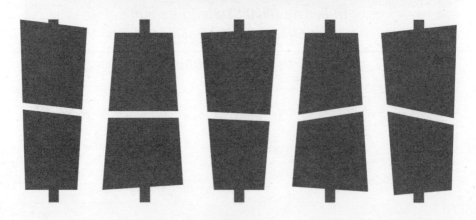

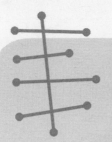

What did the custodian
say when he jumped out
of the closet?

"Supplies!"

Two men are on opposite sides of the river.

*The first man shouts, "How do I get to the other
side of the river?"*

The other man shouts back,
"You ARE on the other side of the river."

What comes once in a minute,
twice in a moment, but never
in a thousand years?

The letter M.

My friend claims he glued himself
to his autobiography.

*I don't believe him, but that's
his story and he's sticking to it.*

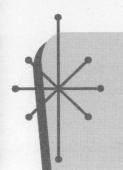

Which American state has the most streets?

Rhode Island.

I tried to start a professional hide-and-seek team, but it didn't work out.

Turns out, good players are hard to find.

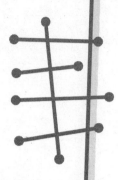

A cruise ship passes by a remote island, and all the passengers see a bearded man running around and waving his arms wildly. "Captain," one passenger asks, "who is that man over there?"

"I have no idea," the Captain replies, "but he goes nuts every year when we pass him."

I asked this girl to meet me at the gym but she never showed up.

I guess the two of us aren't going to work out.

One vowel saves the other vowel's life.

The other vowel says,
"Aye E, I owe you."

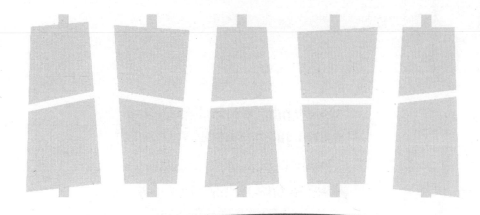

I once hired a limo but when it arrived, the guy driving it walked off! I said "Excuse me? Are you not going to drive it?"

He replied that the price didn't include a driver... so I'd spent $400 on a limo and had nothing to chauffeur it!

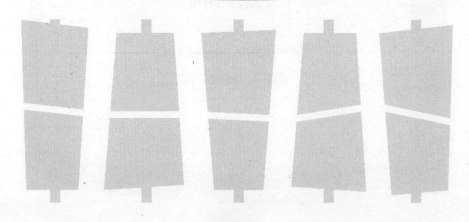

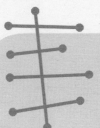

My grandpa warned people the Titanic would sink... No one listened, but he kept warning them until they got sick of him and kicked him out of the cinema.

I read that by law you must turn on your headlights when it's raining in Sweden.

How am I supposed to know when it is raining in Sweden?

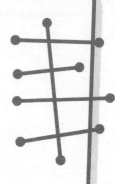

"Poor old thing," thought the man as he watched an older man fishing in a puddle outside a pub. He invited the older man inside for a drink, and asked, "So how many have you caught?"

The older man replied, "You're the eighth today."

I just looked at my ceiling.

I am not sure if it is the best ceiling in the world but it is definitely up there.

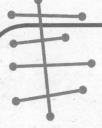

Went to the doctor with a suspicious-looking mole.

He said they all look that way and I should have left him in the garden.

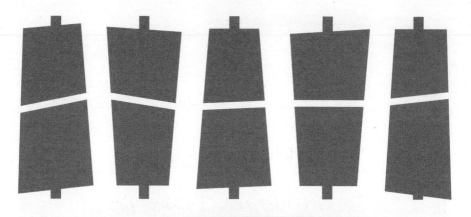

A piece of string is kicked out of a bar, disguises itself and walks back in. "Hey, weren't you that piece of string who was in here before? asked the barman.

"No, I'm a frayed knot!"

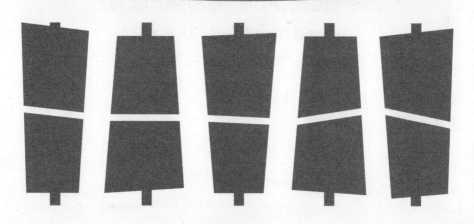

Some jump leads walked into a bar.

The bartender said, "I'll serve you,
but don't start anything."

I saw this advert in a window that said:
"Television for sale, $1, volume
stuck on full."

I thought, "I can't turn that down."

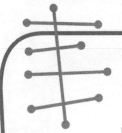

Engineers have made a car
that can run on mint.

*Hopefully, they can make
buses and trains run
on thyme.*

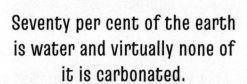

Seventy per cent of the earth
is water and virtually none of
it is carbonated.

So the earth is, in fact, flat.

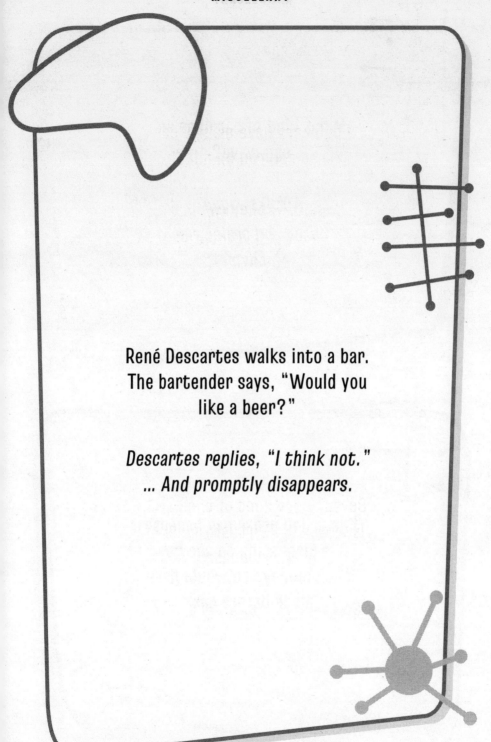

René Descartes walks into a bar.
The bartender says, "Would you
like a beer?"

Descartes replies, "I think not."
... And promptly disappears.

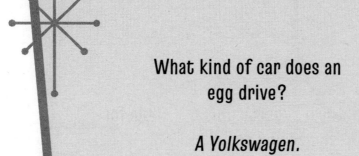

What kind of car does an
egg drive?

A Yolkswagen.

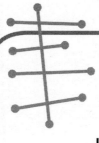

It's called gross pay because
it's disgusting to see how
much money you would have
made before tax.

Plagiarism is getting into trouble for something you didn't do.

Why did the iPad go to the dentist?

It had Bluetooth.

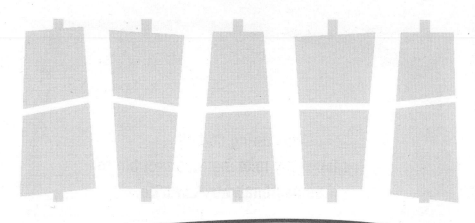

I asked the gym instructor if he could teach me to do the splits. He replied, "How flexible are you?"

I replied, "I can't make it on Tuesdays."

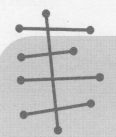

I was going to tell a
carpentry joke but I couldn't
find any that wood work.

Learn to spell...

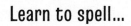

*AutoCorrect isn't always
write.*

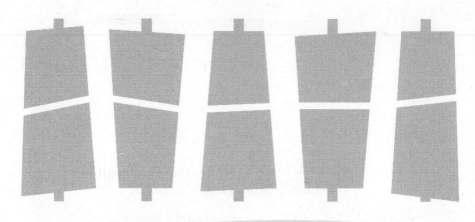

A man walks into a bar with a newt on his shoulder. The bartender says, "What an interesting pet, what's his name?"

"Tiny" the man replies.
"Why do you call him Tiny?"
"Because... He's my newt."

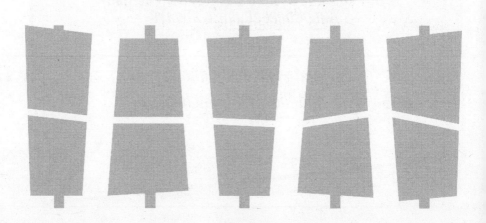

I like what mechanics wear... overall.

Did you know that Davy Crockett had
three ears?

*His left ear, his right ear,
and his wild frontier.*

The fact that Head & Shoulders doesn't have a body wash called Knees & Toes disappoints me.

Did you hear that George got a new job working for Old Macdonald?

He's the new C-I-E-I-O.

My son was spending too much time playing computer games, so I said, "Son, when Abraham Lincoln was your age he was studying books by the light of the fire."

He considered this for a moment and replied, "Dad, when Abraham Lincoln was your age he was President of the United States."

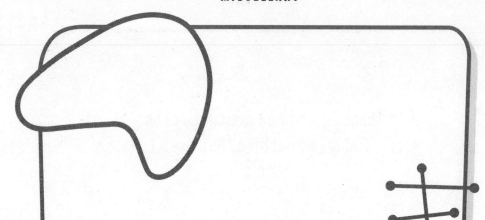

An Englishman, an Irishman, and a Scotsman walk into a bar. The bartender turns to them and says...

"What is this, some kind of joke?"

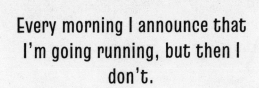

Every morning I announce that I'm going running, but then I don't.

It's a bit of a running joke.

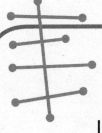

I dreamed about drowning in an ocean made of orange soda last night.

It took me a while to work out it was just a Fanta sea.

Knock knock
Who's there?
Cow goes
Cow goes who?
No silly, Cow goes moo!

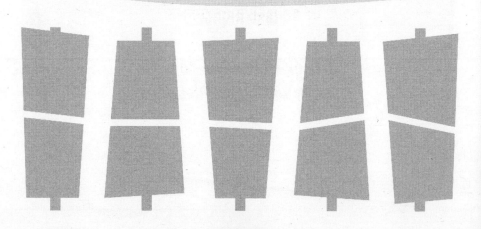

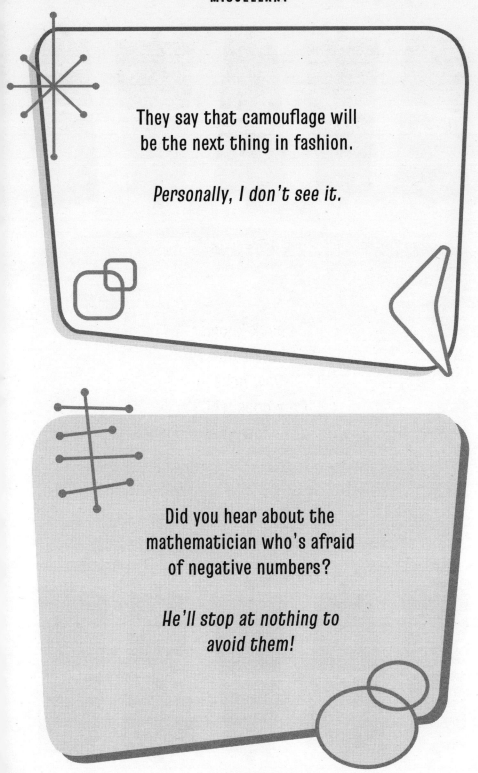

They say that camouflage will be the next thing in fashion.

Personally, I don't see it.

Did you hear about the mathematician who's afraid of negative numbers?

He'll stop at nothing to avoid them!

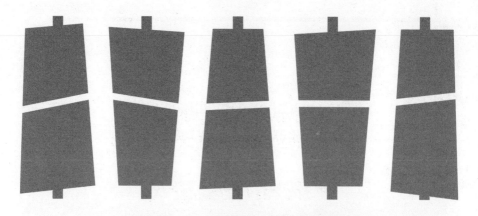

My wife told me to take the spider
out rather than killing him. Went out,
had a few drinks.

Nice guy, turns out he's a
web designer.

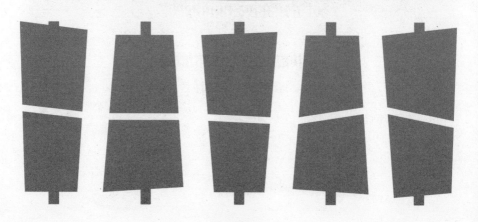

I told my wife she should embrace her mistakes.

She gave me a hug.

What do you say to the triangle player after the concert?

Thanks for every ting.

A man is walking in the desert with his horse and his dog when the dog says, "I can't do this. I need water." The man says, "I didn't know dogs could talk."

The horse replies, "Me neither!"

Which part of your body is the
most musical?

*Your nose because you can pick it
and you can blow it.*

I went to the library and asked if they
had any books on paranoia.

*The librarian replied, "Yes, they're
right behind you!"*

I am such a good singer that people always ask me to sing solo. Solo that they can't hear me. Sometimes they'll even ask me to sing tenor.

Tenor twelve miles away, that is.

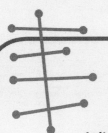

What's the difference between
a dad joke and a bad joke?

*The first letter faces a
different direction.*

What did the judge say to
the dentist?

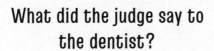

*"Do you swear to pull the
tooth, the whole tooth, and
nothing but the tooth?"*

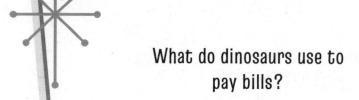

What do dinosaurs use to
pay bills?

Tyrannosaurus checks.

We all know about Murphy's Law:
anything that can go wrong will
go wrong.

But have you heard of Cole's Law?
It's thinly sliced cabbage.

I startled the man next-door with my new electric power tool.

I had to calm him down by saying "Don't worry, it's just a drill!"

I asked the librarian if she knew of any authors who wrote dinosaur novels.

She said, "Try Sarah Topps."

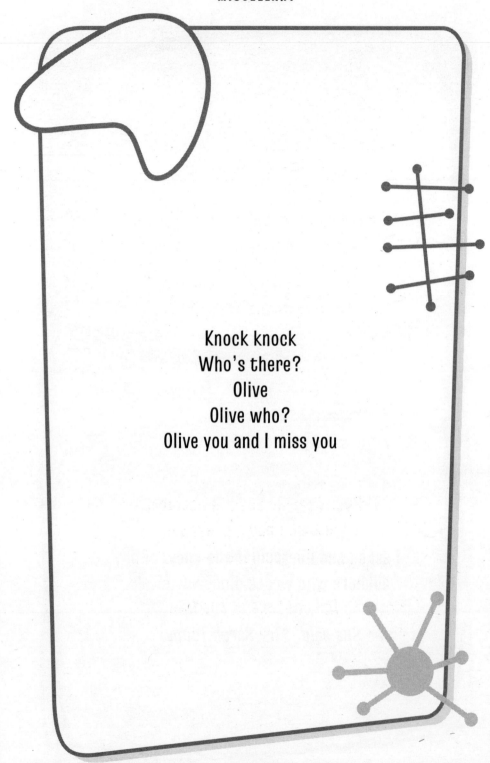

Knock knock
Who's there?
Olive
Olive who?
Olive you and I miss you

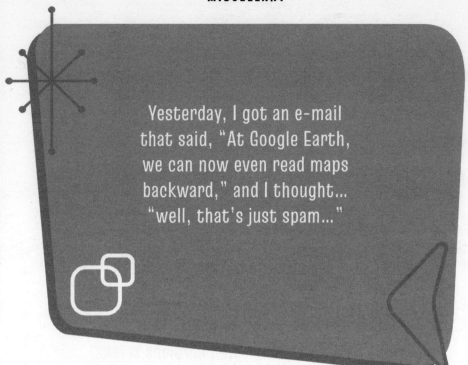

Yesterday, I got an e-mail that said, "At Google Earth, we can now even read maps backward," and I thought... "well, that's just spam..."

I've recently been in hospital because I had a peekaboo accident.

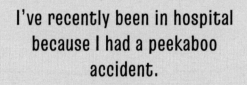

They put me in the ICU.

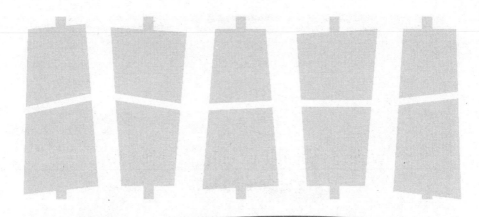

Joe: What does your father do for a living?
Jon: He's a magician. He performs tricks,
like sawing people in half.
Joe: Do you have any brothers or sisters?
Jon: Yep, four half-sisters and a
half-brother.

What do you get when you cross a fish
and an elephant?

Swimming trunks.

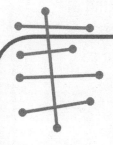

My dentist pulled out the
wrong tooth.

He said it was acci-dental.

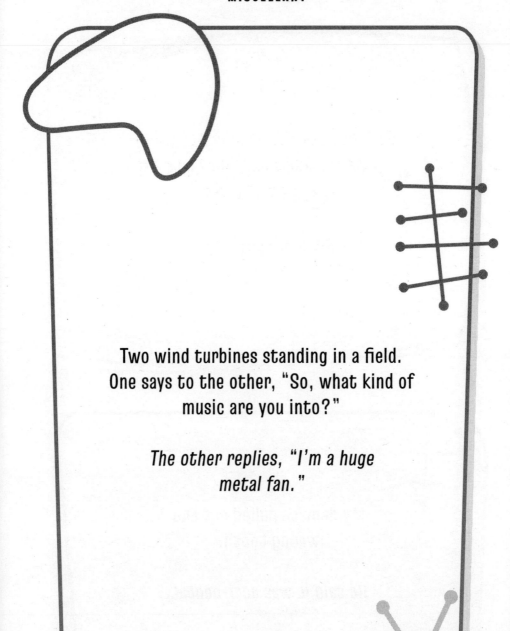

Two wind turbines standing in a field. One says to the other, "So, what kind of music are you into?"

The other replies, "I'm a huge metal fan."

Cowboys used to hang lanterns on
their saddles to guide their
way home at night.

*It was an early form of
saddle-light navigation!*

Mountains aren't just funny.

They're hill-areas.

I went to the doctor about my recent ear problems. He said, "Can you describe the symptoms?"

"What ...?" I said, "Well, Homer's an interesting guy and Marge has blue hair."

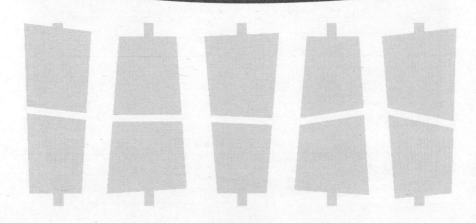

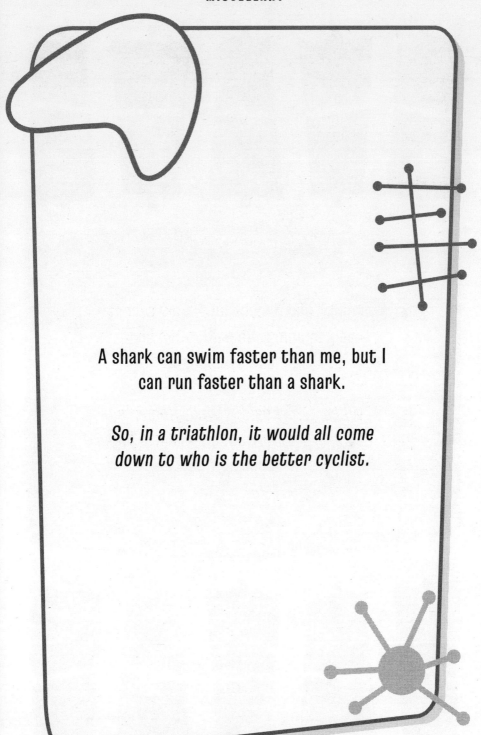

A shark can swim faster than me, but I can run faster than a shark.

So, in a triathlon, it would all come down to who is the better cyclist.

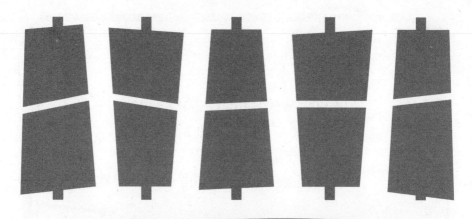

I said to my wife, "Did you know Old McDonald's farm has been taken over by Artificial Intelligence?"
Her: AI?
Me: AI.
Her: Oh.

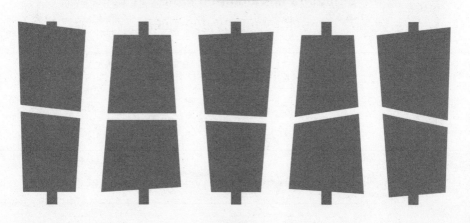

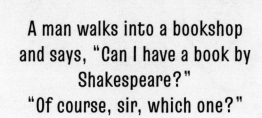

A man walks into a bookshop
and says, "Can I have a book by
Shakespeare?"
"Of course, sir, which one?"

"William."

I woke up this morning to find that
someone had dumped a load of Lego
bricks on my doorstep.

I don't know what to make of it.

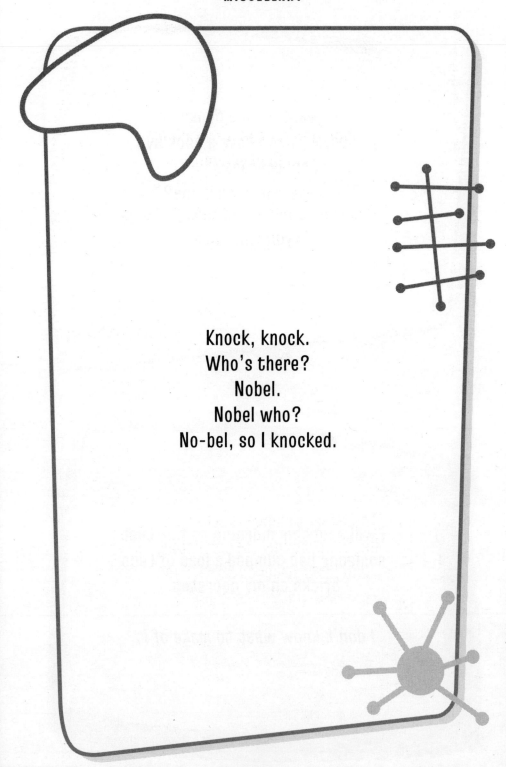

Knock, knock.
Who's there?
Nobel.
Nobel who?
No-bel, so I knocked.

You don't need a parachute
to go skydiving.

*But you do need a parachute to go
skydiving twice.*

The evening news is when they
begin by saying "good evening"
and then proceed to tell you
why it isn't.

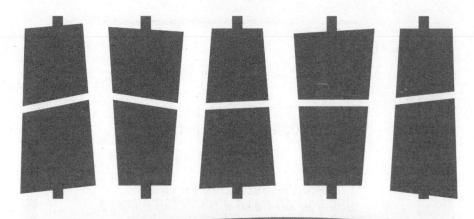

Policeman: "I am arresting you for downloading the entire Wikipedia."

Me: "Wait! I can explain everything!"

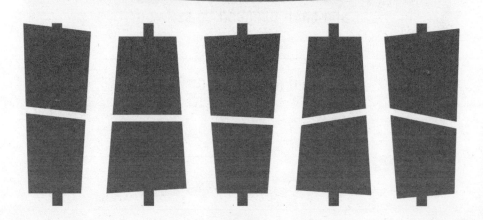

My son turned four today. I didn't recognize him.

I had never seen him be four.

Computer: Choose a password.
Me: hi-hat.
Computer: Password cannot contain symbols.

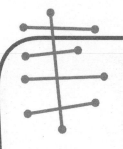

My daughter was doing
history homework and
asked me what I knew
about Galileo.

*I said, "He was a poor boy
from a poor family..."*

My geography teacher asked me if I could
name a country with no R in it.

I said, "No way."

"I just realized that the word 'seven' has 'even' in it."

"That's odd!"

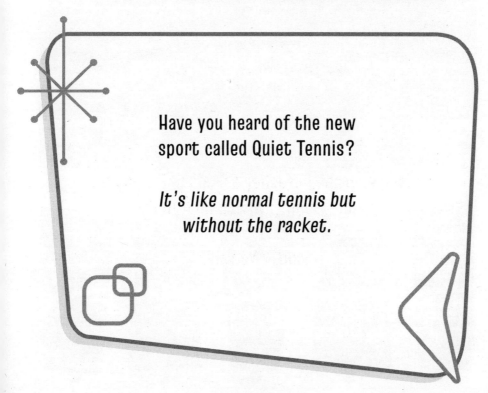

Have you heard of the new sport called Quiet Tennis?

It's like normal tennis but without the racket.

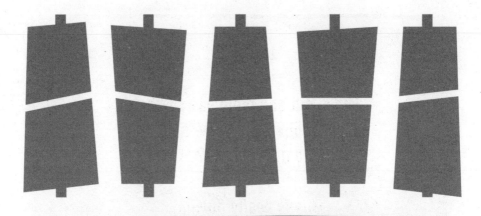

"Dad, are bugs good to eat?" asked the boy.
"Let's not talk about such things at the
dinner table, son," his father replied.
After dinner the father asked, "Now, son,
what did you want to ask me?"
"Oh, nothing," the boy said. "There was a
bug in your soup, but it's gone now."

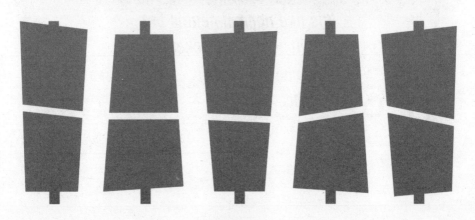

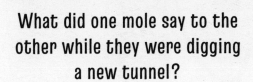

What did one mole say to the other while they were digging a new tunnel?

This is really boring.

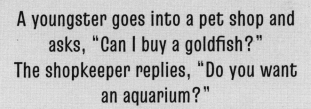

A youngster goes into a pet shop and asks, "Can I buy a goldfish?" The shopkeeper replies, "Do you want an aquarium?"

"No," said the youngster, "I don't care what star sign it is."

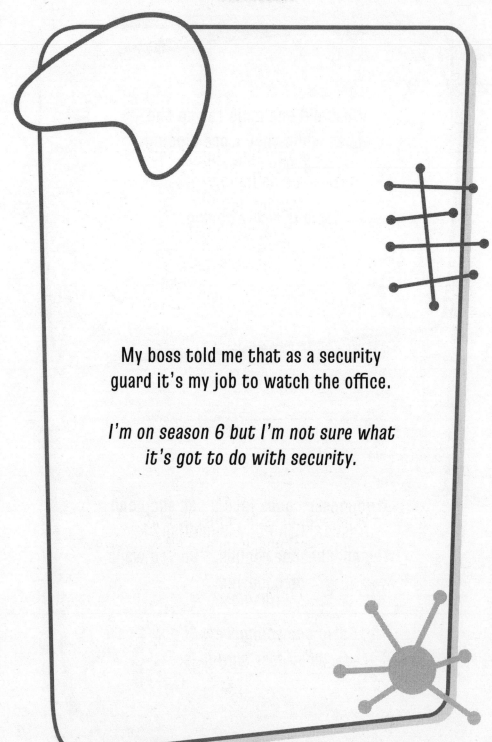

My boss told me that as a security
guard it's my job to watch the office.

*I'm on season 6 but I'm not sure what
it's got to do with security.*

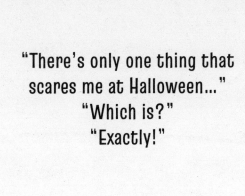

"There's only one thing that
scares me at Halloween..."
"Which is?"
"Exactly!"

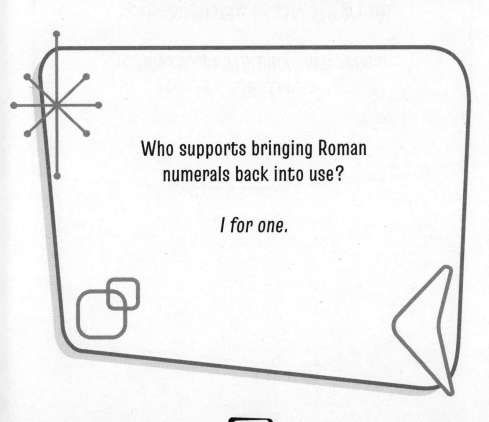

Who supports bringing Roman
numerals back into use?

I for one.

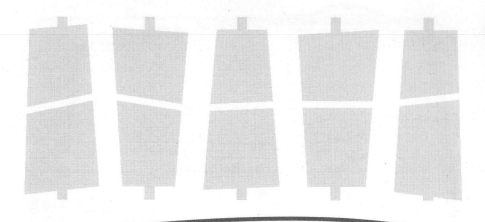

I went into the store and asked, "Can I have a bottle of shampoo please?" The woman replied, "Extra volume?"

"CAN I HAVE A BOTTLE OF SHAMPOO PLEASE?"

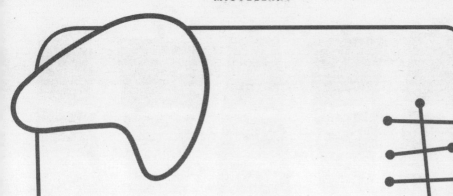

A man goes into a lawyer's office and asks the lawyer: "Excuse me, how much do you charge?"
The lawyer responds: "I charge $1,000 to answer three questions."
"That's expensive isn't it?"

"Yes. And what's your third question?"

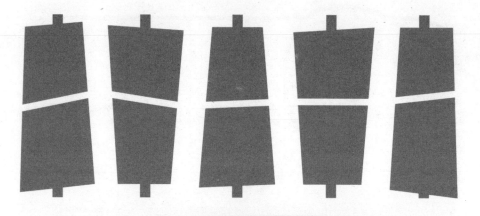

Sylvester Stallone wants to make a film about classical music. He says, "I will be Beethoven."

Jean-Claude van Damme replies, "OK, I'll be Mozart."

Arnold Schwarzenegger says, "I'll be Bach."

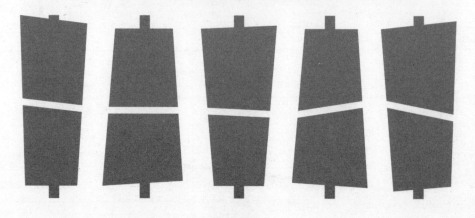